STRAIGHT SPEAKING
FOR AFRICA

BY THE SAME AUTHOR

Le Manguier, le fleuve et la souris (The Mango Tree, the River and the Mouse), published in French by Éditions Jean-Claude Lattès, 1997.

First published in France in 2009 by Michel Lafon
First published in the United States in 2009 by Africa World Press

ISBN: 978-159221-740-3

Africa World Press, Inc.

| P.O. Box 1892 |  | P.O. Box 48 |
| Trenton, NJ 08607 | | Asmara, ERITREA |

DENIS SASSOU NGUESSO

STRAIGHT SPEAKING
FOR AFRICA

Interviews with Edouard Dor

Preface by NELSON MANDELA

Africa World Press, Inc.

P.O. Box 1892
Trenton, NJ 08607

P.O. Box 48
Asmara, ERITREA

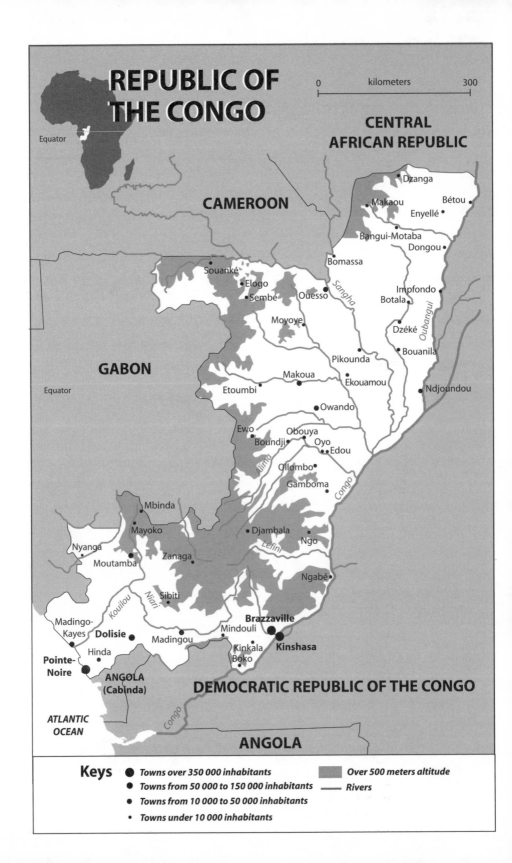

REPUBLIC OF THE CONGO

0   kilometers   300

Equator

CENTRAL AFRICAN REPUBLIC

CAMEROON

• Dzanga

• Makaou   Bétou •

Enyellé •

Bangui-Motaba •

Bomassa •   Dongou •

Souanké •

• Elogo   Ouesso •   Impfondo •

• Sembé   Botala •

Moyoye •   Dzéké •

Bouanila •

Pikounda •

GABON   Makoua •   Ndjoundou •

Etoumbi •   Ekouamou •

Equator   Owando •

Ewo •   Obouya •

Boundji •   Oyo •• Edou

Ollombo •

Gamboma •

Mbinda •

Mayoko •   Djambala •   Ngo •

Nyanga •   Zanaga •

Moutamba •

Sibiti •   Ngabé •

Madingo-   **Brazzaville**
Kayes •   **Dolisie**   Mindouli •
Hinda •   Madingou •   Kinkala •   **Kinshasa**
Boko •
**Pointe-
Noire**   ANGOLA
(Cabinda)   **DEMOCRATIC REPUBLIC OF THE CONGO**

*ATLANTIC
OCEAN*

ANGOLA

Keys
● *Towns over 350 000 inhabitants*   *Over 500 meters altitude*
● *Towns from 50 000 to 150 000 inhabitants*   *Rivers*
• *Towns from 10 000 to 50 000 inhabitants*
· *Towns under 10 000 inhabitants*

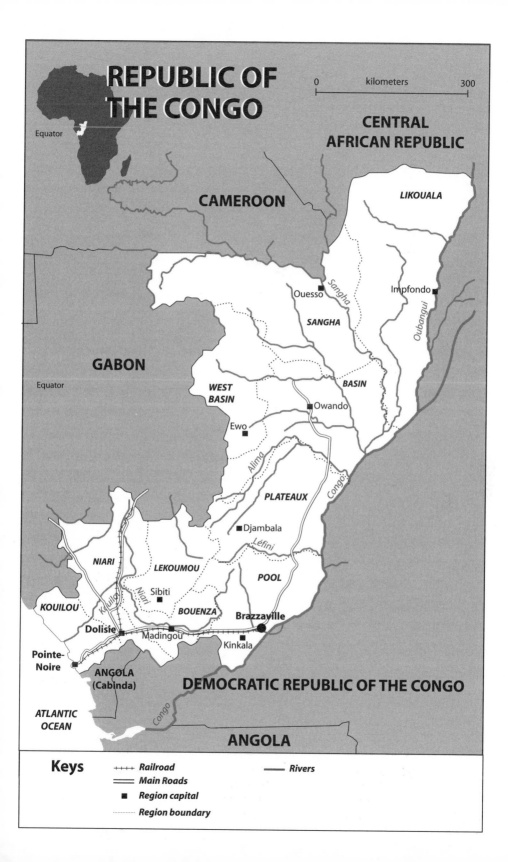

REPUBLIC OF THE CONGO

0   kilometers   300

Equator

CENTRAL AFRICAN REPUBLIC

CAMEROON

LIKOUALA

Ouesso

Impfondo

SANGHA

GABON

Equator

WEST BASIN

BASIN

Owando

Ewo

Alima

Congo

PLATEAUX

Djambala

Léfini

NIARI

LEKOUMOU

POOL

Niari

Kouilou

Sibiti

BOUENZA

Brazzaville

KOUILOU

Dolisie

Madingou

Kinkala

Pointe-Noire

ANGOLA (Cabinda)

DEMOCRATIC REPUBLIC OF THE CONGO

ATLANTIC OCEAN

Congo

ANGOLA

Keys

+++++ Railroad
===== Main Roads
■ Region capital
·········· Region boundary

——— Rivers

To my darling daughter, Edith Lucie
To my friend, Nelson Mandela

CONTENTS

PREFACE
by
NELSON MANDELA

In President Denis Sassou Nguesso, I recognise a man who is not only one of our great African leaders – one who has presided over the Organisation of African Unity – but also one of those who gave their unconditional support to our fighters' demand for freedom, and who worked tirelessly to free oppressed peoples from their chains and help restore their dignity and hope.

We will never forget his constant efforts in favour of the liberation of the peoples of Southern Africa. We will never forget the negotiator who hosted the Brazzaville international conference that led to the independence of Namibia, as well as the recognition of the ANC by the apartheid regime and the freeing of all its prisoners. It is also to that man that I pay tribute.

NELSON MANDELA

(Cape Town, 1996)

– FOREWORD –

Why this book ?

Why this book ? I am immediately tempted to answer that while I am a public figure and it is quite proper that I and my commitments, life, activities, ideas and policies should be subject to scrutiny, I have observed that what is said and written about me is not always scrupulously truthful. I have certainly done some positive things and, no doubt, some less positive things, like any political leader or human being. Like any human being, I would like others to listen to me, and like any political leader, I would like to be understood. I am convinced that this can only be achieved by following the path of truth.

That is why I thought a book – a lasting record – would be the best way of providing my account, my truth, for those who know or wish to know me.

I decided this account should be in dialogue form because I wished to give answers on every last point and wanted the discussion to be based on genuine, direct questions. It was. I was also keen to talk to someone

17

curious, who would do their best to understand rather than judge. Someone I could look in the eye. After all, is that not the best way to examine our life, by seeing it reflected in the eye of another?

DENIS SASSOU NGUESSO

Brazzaville, May 2009

– PART ONE –

HUNTING BUFFALO WITH AN ASSEGAI

The scene of a happy childhood

— Perhaps we can begin this interview logically at the beginning, President, by talking about your birthplace, Edou, a little village in the centre of the Congo.

When I was born in 1943, my native village, Edou, was much larger than today. Over the years, migration to the cities has drained off a good part of its population, a phenomenon that has affected many of our villages. In the colonial period, Edou was the administrative centre of a canton, with its clinic, little maternity hospital and school, which was quite a lot in those days. The administrator even had a residence there, which seemed like a little palace to us children. A visit from him was a great event. The youngest of us caught chickens and goat kids for the meals. Yes, I saw all colonial life unfolding before my eyes when I was young.

— The positive sides, but negative ones too ?

Especially the forced labour.

— Forced labour ?

Yes. Road building, for instance. Every year, they took away our mothers for a month, while we children stayed in the village. All day, our mothers carried heavy baskets filled with earth. Then our fathers and brothers were sometimes sent a hundred kilometres away to build bridges or housing for colonial civil servants.

— What kind of man was your father ?

My father was one of the village clan chiefs. He was a very hard-working man, highly respected among the M'Bochis [1], and a great hunter. He used to bring down buffalo with an assegai spear, that was how intrepid he was ! He was a tracker too. He would follow the trail of herds of buffalo or packs of wild boar for dozens of kilometres, then return to fetch the villagers when he found the animals. I remember the children taking part in these hunts. As soon as news of a herd came in, the teacher stopped his lesson so we could go with

1. An ethnic group inhabiting the centre and north of the country.

the hunters and act as beaters. We climbed into the trees where we were safe from any charge. When the signal was given, we began to shout to frighten the animals and make them run towards the hunters. My father would lead the hunt deep in the forest. It was a true battle!

My father wasn't just brave, though, he was an honest, upright man too, like all the people of the village. In those days, we didn't know what a key was for in our region, simply because we never locked our doors. When someone went on a journey, they closed the door of their home and put a plank across the outside to stop it coming open. That was all. No lock, no key and no thefts ever reported.

— *What about your mother?*

I think I was her favourite. Of course, I was her youngest child and the youngest are always a treated a little like only sons. I drank her milk to the last drop, she never stopped feeding me! She was a very calm woman. Hard-working too, and silent : she didn't talk.

— *Did you get your composure from her?*

Absolutely. She wasn't a quarrelsome woman looking for trouble. She was very level-headed and upright.

— How did she react when you became President of the Republic ?

This will surprise you : she stayed in the village ! She wasn't about to leave her rural life just because her son had become President. I don't even remember her visiting the presidential residence in Brazzaville more than four times. She didn't ask to come. To give you an idea of how little she cared for pomp and privilege, when she died, the few small sums I'd sent her were found in her belongings. She hadn't touched the money, she felt she didn't need it. The clearest memory I have of her is when I went on an official presidential visit to Oyo, where she then lived. She didn't attend the official assembly. She preferred to wait for me under the great tree that casts a little shade on our family home. When I arrived, she was sitting there with her woman friends. She got up when she saw me and hugged and kissed me, then sat back down and pulled me to her, sitting me on her lap. I was in paratrooper's uniform and I was President of the Republic ! At that moment, though, I was mainly my mother's darling son. Do you know what I regret most today when I think of that scene ? That no-one was there to take a photograph. I regret that a lot.

– 2 –

A HUNDRED-KILOMETRE WALK
TO SCHOOL

Initiation – A first success – Middle school

— In our childhood and teenage years, we've all had what you might call "great moments": events that shape us and help us grow up, events that stay with us for life and make us what we are. What were yours?

I can say there were three great moments in my childhood and teenage years, three moments that were formative and even decisive for my education, and which certainly left their mark. In any case, they were partly responsible for making me the adult I later became. The first great moment occurred in my village, Edou. It was my initiation. I hadn't yet started school. I was perhaps five or six. I'm not sure about my age because there were no registries in our villages at the time. The year of my birth was declared as 1943, but it may have been 1942. Anyway, one day, my father and his friends decided I should be initiated.

25

— For what reasons ? Not everyone in the village was initiated.

I don't really know why I was chosen. In fact, I wasn't allowed to know. What I do know is that those who were initiated — adults, young people or even children like me — weren't chosen at random.

— But looking back, can't you see why ? Did you have some outstanding characteristic at the time ? For instance, a certain influence over your friends or your brothers and sisters despite your very young age ?

No, I don't think so. I was the youngest of my family, so I can't say I had any sort of authority over my brothers and sisters. I may have been a little more astute.

— How were you initiated ?

That's not something we talk about. Initiation must remain a mystery, that's the condition for its survival. No initiate must confide in the uninitiated. When a chief dies, rituals of every kind are performed in closed circles in the village. At these times, a number of people are selected for initiation, either because they've asked to be initiated, or because the elders have chosen them. These people, destined to become *mwené*, or "men of honour", enter the circle of initiates. Over a number of years, they're taught by the most experienced, oldest men. For instance, you're taught how and on what occasions the elders organise their consultations, how and why they make decisions, how they manage questions of public policy, and so on.

— *How can a child of five or six learn all these things ?*

They don't tell you everything, obviously ! But even as a child, you're aware that you're part of a closed circle and you clearly understand that it's a privilege. Naturally, at five or six, you don't really grasp that being an initiate involves certain responsibilities, but I can assure you that you come to realise it quite soon enough as you grow up.

— *What was the second great moment of your childhood ?*

After my first years of lessons at my village primary school, my teacher spoke to my father and insisted I should continue my education. This meant I had to go to the middle school in Owando, the provincial administrative centre a hundred kilometres from Edou. A hundred kilometres meant a two-day walk, fifty kilometres a day ! My mother put up the most resistance. She couldn't bear the idea of her youngest son leaving her and going so far away. On the day I left, she followed me down the road, unable to say goodbye. After two kilometres, I — all of ten years old — had to reassure her and tell her to go home, that everything would be alright. I had to make this journey a number of times each year, since I returned to the village during each holiday period – Christmas and Easter. I must say those long days spent walking were very formative. It took a lot of determination and endurance.

— *Where did you stay in Owando ?*

We could sleep in the school.

— *Only sleep ?*

Yes. For the rest – for meals, essentially – we had to manage with the little money our parents gave us and whatever we could find for ourselves in Owando, especially fish that we caught.

— *A tough life for children !*

Yes. Four of the six schoolchildren from Edou gave up and went home to the village. They couldn't take the harsh life there. Oddly, it was the oldest children who threw in the towel.

— *Who were your teachers at the time ? Were they French ?*

At primary school, all the masters were African. Some of them came from a long way off. In the second and third years, our master was a Central African from Bangui. Back then, the colonial authorities deliberately moved civil servants all round French Equatorial Africa and. they accepted it. Congolese teachers were posted to Chad – for instance, the future President Massemba-Débat, who taught in Fort-Lamy, now N'Djamena. At middle school, our master was Gabonese. I should point out that all these teachers were very conscientious and thorough. I have very clear memories of those people. They gave us an extremely solid education.

– *They taught you the history and geography of France, rather than the Congo.*

That's true. At middle school, I really noticed how little the content of some lessons had to do with our real lives. We were supposed to have a detailed knowledge of the rivers and mountains of France, yet we knew virtually nothing about the geography of the Middle Congo, the land of our ancestors, where we lived.

– *Weren't some of the seeds of African nationalism sown in the lessons given to those young people : a history that wasn't theirs and the geography of a country that wasn't theirs ?*

Absolutely, but not just in the lessons on a history or geography that wasn't theirs. Many students also realised that the very development planned for the colonies had nothing to do with the country's real needs. It was an exploitation economy. The roads that were built by local labour weren't designed to facilitate travel and trade within the country, but primarily to transport raw materials and goods to be shipped to Metropolitan France. A certain elite was given instruction and training, but not for its own betterment, rather to oversee the population. Healthcare wasn't intended to make the people healthier for their benefit, but mainly so they could work harder for the coloniser. This was no endogenous development reflecting the needs of our country ! All Congolese students were well aware of this at the time.

— *So what was the third and last formative event in your youth ?*

I must have been twelve or thirteen. I remember it was a September morning and our whole family had gone fishing not far from the village. It was a fine day and the fish were biting. Suddenly, we heard a commotion. A gendarme was heading over, accompanied by a guide and a few villagers. We hadn't seen a gendarme in our village for weeks and they never brought good news. Seeing my father looking anxious, this particular gendarme quickly reassured him. "It's nothing serious," he said. "Is the young Denis Sassou here ?" I was completely focused on my fishing, my feet planted in the mud of the river. "My son's over there !" answered my father, pointing at me. "Well," continued the gendarme, "I have a letter for him. He's passed his secondary-school entrance exam with flying colours. Congratulations !" Our sudden joy was mixed with relief. The fishing excursion ended immediately. As you can well imagine, celebrations were in order back in the village !

So I was one of the first thirty young people selected by entrance examination that year to continue my education at one of the four secondary schools in the Middle Congo. I would begin a five-year course of studies at the Dolisie secondary school in the Niari region in the south of the country, which would lead on to a career as a teacher, with status, a salary and the respect of my fellow countrymen. I saw this as a real success, firstly because the entrance examination was very selective, and secondly, more importantly, because it was a reward for all the hard work I'd put in over the last two years. It meant that the long marches, the months spent away from my family and the hardship hadn't been for nothing ! After celebrating my success, my parents got to work and almost emptied the little village shop to kit me out. They even bought me a pair of slippers !

— *I suppose it was quite an event when you left your village for the city ?*

How right you are ! It was a whole series of firsts for me ! I climbed into the cab of a lorry for the first time, which was a privilege. It took me to Owando, then to Makoua, where a small plane belonging to the colonial administration landed once a week. Obviously, this was the first time I'd flown. When I arrived in Brazzaville, my brothers were there to welcome me. It was the first time I'd seen Brazzaville ! We took a taxi, another first for me, and crossed the city to the railway station, where I caught my first train : the great *Congo-Océan* travelling to Dolisie. The school was six or seven kilometres from the station and a coach came to pick up the pupils and take them there. It was the first time I'd been on a coach ! At school, we were very strictly supervised and the training was very thorough. There were thirty of us at the start of the course. More than half failed to finish the five years of study.

— *That's where you got to know teachers from France ?*

Yes. That was a first too !

– 3 –

CHOOSING THE ARMY
A providential meeting – A destiny

– Did you develop a close relationship with any of your teachers at secondary school, especially the French ones ?

It was difficult. Most of them had something of a colonial attitude. The one exception was Maurice Spindler from the Haute-Savoie region of France, who was different. He was our friend and we were close. He spoke up for us in staff meetings. He was our one-man union ! At the end of my programme of studies, he thought I was too young to finish school and felt I should carry on to baccalaureate level and beyond. He thought my leaving was a waste and wanted to do something about it. But what ? This was 1960, 1961, and France's former African colonies were independent. He told me : "You have to go to Brazzaville with your reports and apply there. You're a top student here, I can't see why they wouldn't take you. No arguments, you have to continue your education !"

So I went from Dolisie to Brazzaville. Other young people from different regions were making the same move to the capital and I learned about another side of life there : string-pulling. I discovered that a certain number of pupils were given places in teaching establishments through political recommendation. I was the top student in my year at school, but I was refused a place because I had no sponsor. That was the first great disappointment in my life.

However, Maurice Spindler told me not to give up hope. He was convinced that if I persisted, I'd succeed in the end. Then he read in the newspaper about an entrance examination organised by the government. Its aim was to recruit young people with a certain level of education, train them and then commission them as officers in our new national army. It was an accelerated six-month training course run by the French army in Bouar in the Central African Republic for the first future army officers of recently independent African countries. "Enter the exam," Spindler told me, "and you'll be able to continue to study, even though it's a different form of education in the army. Then you'll be in the front line to serve your country." He dictated my application and I sat the exam. It was an essay on : "The role of the army in the institution of national unity". Mine was the best paper !

— After those six months of training, when you became an NCO and qualified as a paratrooper, you entered the Combined Reserve Officers School at Cherchell, to the west of Algiers.

That was in 1961-1962, at the end of the Algerian War. During my time at that military school, I saw something of the disorder in the French Army, with the supporters of General de Gaulle pitted against those who were fiercely opposed to Algerian independence. I returned to the Congo with the rank of second lieutenant, then chose to go and round off my military training in France at the Infantry Application School in Saint-Maixent, Poitou-Charentes. At the end of my time there, I was congratulated by the commanding officer. Back in Brazzaville, I was assigned to work with Captain Marien Ngouabi to found the Congolese First Airborne Group, whose role would be to spearhead our new army. So it was at this point that I met that young officer, who had studied at Saint-Cyr. He had already begun to think seriously about political issues and would later rise to the highest office in the country.

— You then rose through the ranks.

Yes, I was successively commissioned lieutenant, captain, commander of a paratroop corps – an elite unit – for seven years, then Commander of the

Military Zone of Brazzaville, Commander of Land Forces, Director-General of State Security, and finally Minister of Defence from 1975 to 1979. I held those final responsibilities under President Marien Ngouabi.

– 4 –

THE COMMUNIST OPTION

Political commitment
– The communist experiment –
Presidents of the Congo

*— At what point did your military career turn to political
commitment ?*

In fact, my political commitment predated my
joining the army. As I've said, like my classmates,
I became aware of my country's problems back at
secondary school : colonial exploitation and the
scant benefits it offered to the population, not to
mention the all too frequent denial of freedoms.
At the time, we were student-union activists, working with our elders in France, whose political thinking was more advanced and perhaps more
sophisticated. The Association of Congolese Students in France strongly influenced our political
perceptions, as did the Federation of Students of
Black Africa in France. A lot of these young people
met up again in the army at a time when they were

already developing a structured political philosophy.

— *Why did you choose Marxism-Leninism ?*

You actually have to bear in mind that the Cold War was at its height then. The world was divided into two hostile — even enemy — blocs, and the only allies of our third-world countries in their liberation struggles at the time were the countries of the Communist Bloc. For instance, the peoples of Angola, Mozambique, Guinea-Bissau and Cape Verde were fighting the troops of the Portuguese coloniser supported by the West. The only aid these peoples received was from the Soviet Union, China and Cuba. That's what determined our choices as future leaders of Africa, far more than strict Marxist ideology, obviously.

— *Because there weren't any other choices, in fact.*

Yes, we didn't actually have a wide range of choices.

— *Even so, communism existed in Africa before the word was invented.*

Yes, life in Africa is communal. Sharing is essential. You know what the idea of family means in our lands. It takes in far more people than in Europe, including cousins, distant cousins, friends, allies, friends of friends, and so on. Visitors are always welcome and anyone in distress will always find help when they step across the threshold of an African hut or house, wherever it is.

— Even though the aid the communist countries provided to support liberation struggles in Africa may have been vital, wasn't the communist system a genuine handicap for the development of the Congo ?

It's true that it was a very cumbersome system and the inertia of the bureaucracy in particular had a disproportionate impact. However, it must be said that the communist system was wrongly applied, even in the countries of Eastern Europe. We only have to look at the results : all the communist regimes collapsed one after another, and China, still ruled by a communist party, is developing today because it decided to join the capital-intensive world economy, turning away from the practices dictated by Marxism-Leninism. So if the system didn't work in Eastern Europe, how could you expect it to work elsewhere ? Also, if such a system is to be implemented, it has to be accompanied by a sufficiently high level of political consciousness among the population. People don't have the same attitude towards public things as they do towards private ones. Let me give you a simple example : you won't pay the same attention to or take the same care of the car you drive if it belongs to the State rather than to you. Well, the same type of behaviour can be observed on a broader scale. When dealing with public things, people don't have the same level of conscientiousness or the same determination to succeed. It's as if it were something foreign to them, although the issue is quite simply one of the most basic public-spiritedness, that's to say the best way of living together to ensure everyone's well-being and happiness ! At the time, we suffered a number of setbacks and disappointments : overstaffing leading to inefficiency, favouritism and pork-barrel politics, not to mention administrative errors due to obvious incompetence or serious inexperience. The State intervened in everything, from the organisation of a little farm deep in the country to great industrial projects, including – and I'm not exaggerating here – the running of bakeries ! Obviously, this system of State omnipresence didn't work. Although, to be fair, we must remember there was no private Western investment in the Congo, and if there's no private investment in a country, the State has to intervene in every sector of the economy.

– Did the aid provided by the Soviet Union and China not make up for the lack of support from the West ?

Not at all, or at least not enough. The USSR and China couldn't compensate in every sector. If China offered support in farming or textiles, for instance, it couldn't help us in other areas. The same was true of the Soviet Union.

— One of the lessons of that Marxist-Leninist experiment was perhaps that the ideology and the system that goes with it aren't necessarily suited to the economy of developing nations.

Perhaps. But has anyone really developed an economic system suited to developing nations? That's the question. Capitalism has been hit by a violent crisis, a crisis that's rocking the entire planet, and has proved unreliable, like communism before it. This system too is revealing its weaknesses, shortcomings and limits.

— Since we're talking about difficulties in managing the country, what's your opinion of your predecessors at the head of the Congo? I'm thinking specifically of Father Fulbert Youlou, Alphonse Massemba-Débat and Marien Ngouabi.

I was young when Youlou was the Congo's first President and so – I was going to say "naturally" – opposed to his policies. For the country's young leaders, it seemed to be a continuation of colonialism. Massemba-Débat was different. He was a conscientious man of the Protestant faith and we supported him at the time because we thought he represented progress in relation to Youlou. His way of tackling the country's problems and his management of the State suited us better, but he didn't go far enough in our opinion, so a movement emerged that led to his overthrow and replacement by Marien Ngouabi as President. We wanted to move more quickly to consolidate our political and economic independence.

— *What kind of man was Marien Ngouabi ?*

He was a man of conviction, firmly convinced that the ideas he fought for were sound. He was extremely honest and I believe he essentially did what he rightly or wrongly believed was the proper thing to do.

A VAST OUTLET FOR POLITICAL UNREST

The National Conference
– The multiparty system –
"I accept responsibility" – President Lissouba

– Marien Ngouabi came to power in 1969 and was assassinated eight years later. He was followed by Yhombi-Opango, who remained in power until February 1979, when you became President of the Republic. In 1990, you decided to introduce the multiparty system in the Congo. Reflecting events elsewhere in Africa, you organised a National Conference, beginning in February 1991. Why was that ? Was it because you had no choice ?

To fully understand the complexity of the situation at the time, we have to turn back the clock and put things into perspective. We, the representatives of a single Marxist-Leninist party, were in power, but increasingly conscious that the division of the world into two hostile blocs no longer reflected the geostrategic and economic realities of the day. We were also aware that communism had done more to hinder the development of our country than expedite it. The Central Committee of our organisation, the Congolese Party of Labour, began to examine these issues and especially the fact that we were facing inevitable changes that compelled us to move towards a multiparty system and a truly democratic government. Then, in November 1989, the Berlin Wall fell, at just the right time to confirm our analysis of the situation. There was also the African political context. All over the continent, national conferences were being held with varying degrees of success : in Benin and Gabon, and soon in Togo, Niger, Chad and Zaire. In passing, I should point out that these were essentially French-speaking countries, as if the phenomenon of mimicry in relation to the urgent need for democratic debate only affected French-speaking nations. We'll come back to that.

– *What actually happened in the Congo at that point ?*

We decided to move in stages, since we thought that the great majority of Congolese might not yet be sufficiently prepared to enter into a democratic debate overnight, and that if we were too hasty, it would probably do more harm than good. Don't forget that the Congo was only thirty years old ! Compare that with the history of France and other European countries. How many centuries did it take for democracy to emerge in France, Italy or

Germany ? And governed by what conditions and accompanied by what birth pangs ? So, from November 1989 on, we in the Congo began to draw initial conclusions from the collapse of communism in the countries of Eastern Europe, which we saw as very clear evidence of the failure of the single-party system and State centralism. We recognised that Marxism-Leninism was no longer the right path and we laid the foundations for a multiparty system in June 1990. At the time, we felt a need – and today, history shows we were right – to warn that countries such as ours, with strong ethnic divisions and unequal levels of internal development, were vulnerable, and that the new political parties would have to be mul-tiethnic, and so genuinely representative on a national level and not just a local one. That's why we voted a law specifying that a party would only be officially recognised as a political party if it had leaders from at least five or six different regions of the country.

– *The Congo had already experienced the multiparty system.*

Yes, immediately after independence. At the time, the multiparty system led to very violent clashes, verging on ethnic war.

– *So it was decided to introduce a multiparty system with multiethnic parties.*

Some groups in the country thought this was the wrong choice and claimed there was no reason why a multiparty system with no conditions or restrictions should not be introduced immediately. This faction won over public opinion, supported as it was by aggressive trade-union action that not only completely paralysed the country a number of times, but frankly became almost insurrectional on occasion. Under pressure, we repealed the law that had been passed and decided to apply the principles of the French law of 1901 governing associations to the formation of political parties. Under that law, only three people are needed to set up an association. As a result, there are nearly a hundred and fifty political parties in the Congo today ! Obviously, anyone could set up their own political party and most of them were based on ethnic, clan or even family lines. That was the situation when the national conference began at a virtually insurrectional pace. I was the President of the Republic and posterity would hold me responsible for the country and my fellow citizens. I decided to allow the movement to continue.

— But when you sensed that the discussions at this National Conference were taking a dangerous turn — scores were settled, lies told and hatred fanned in a process that could ultimately lead to tragedy and actually did so in the end — why didn't you say to yourself: "Well, if that's the way it is, I'm leaving. I'm going back to Oyo and they can sort it out between them" ?

That would have been irresponsible of me. My historic duty was to supervise the movement and not to try and check or hinder it in any way. No, the process had to be allowed to reach its conclusion without going seriously astray. I'm still convinced I did the right thing. At the time, Nelson Mandela, who'd finally been freed from prison in South Africa a year before and was still only the vice-President of the ANC[1], was in Brazzaville on an official visit. He told me, "The National Conference is a real danger, but it's a necessary evil. Your opponents will do all they can to turn you into a tyrant. Opinion is fickle, as you know, but you're unassailable. Just hold on ! We'll be there to prevent the worst. You're serving history and that's all that counts !"

— A remarkable message of support ! But did the National Conference help to identify potential partners for dialogue, or was it just an outlet for public opinion ?

That's exactly it : an outlet. This was a serious problem, because the National Conference was actually intended to implement democracy. In fact, listening to the speeches, it was plain that the very people who preached democracy didn't practise it

---

1. The African National Congress, a party founded in 1912, banned from 1960 to 1990 before being authorised again in 1990. It has since become the main political force in South Africa.

Denis Sassou Nguesso

in their own political organisations. None of them were representative and none of them were elected leaders or even designated spokespersons for their movement, which had actually been formed without any preliminary constitutive congress being organised ! They didn't represent a group, community or any political option, only themselves. In fact – and this is another paradox of these discussions, which were supposed to be democratic – the Conference became the preserve of the new orthodoxy ! Only those criticising the regime could express themselves freely. Anyone expressing a different point of view was booed and shouted down. At no point in the Conference was there a genuine democratic debate in which every point of view could be freely expressed, one that would give rise to a few fundamental ideas forming a starting point for reflection. Naturally, some of the people around me saw this agitation as dangerous for the country and wanted to bring it to an end.

I didn't share their opinion. All in all, I believed that we should allow events to follow their course, remaining at the helm to try and channel the movement and prevent it from it taking a dangerous turn if necessary. So I rejected the suggestion that the Conference should be wound up. It was originally planned to last two weeks, but finally went on for three months. At the request of its participants, I regularly issued decrees enabling it to continue. In all this turmoil, I was determined to

48

take full responsibility as Head of State. In fact, that was the title of my address to the nation at the time : *J'assume (I Accept Responsibility)*[1]. I believe that speech is still remembered in the Congo and even beyond.

— *What was your intention when you wrote that declaration ?*

I wanted to give a direction to the National Conference for one reason : so that despite its excesses, it might lead to something tangible ; that something concrete might emerge from the turmoil. I specifically suggested that commissions should be organised to note and collate different opinions, and propose rational choices for the future.

— *At the end of the National Conference, they gave you a Prime Minister.*

Not at all. "Gave" isn't the word for it. The Conference — and that's why I said it was insurrectional in nature — did not "give" the President of the Republic a Prime Minister. The Conference decided to vest *all* executive powers in the Prime Minister — all the powers of the President, including command of the armed forces. The Head of

---

1. The full text of *J'assume (I Accept Responsibility)* is to be found in Appendix I.

State was barely allowed to keep control of foreign relations. That was all.

— Once again, why did you remain in office at that point ? Did you hope to make your Prime Minister see reason ?

Unfortunately, no. I stayed firstly because I was conscious of my responsibilities, and secondly, to see the experiment through to its end. It was not up to me to oppose the majority that was expressing itself at this point and which basically believed it was right. It was not for me alone to stop it, but the democratic process could. I was sure of that. The opposition would have to organise itself and I knew how difficult that would be. In fact, the general election showed that those who were advocating democratic debate were unable to comply with its rules — rules that they themselves had drawn up at the Conference, remember, including the new Constitution ! It was then that the violence began, with Lissouba[1] and even Milongo[2], since both refused to honour the principles they had set for themselves.

— What did you do then ?

---

1. Pascal Lissouba, the President elected in 1992 after the National Conference.
2. André Milongo, the Prime Minister elected by the National Conference.

I was mainly determined that everyone should comply with the democratic process. The National Conference could not be allowed to plunge us into anarchy. My responsibility was to lead our country peacefully and securely until elections were held in which the Congolese people could express their will. That is why I remained in office, come what may ! I also decided to take part in the electoral process with my party, the Congolese Party of Labour (PCT). There was no question of winding it up : it was a party like the others, with quite strong support in the Congo. So the PCT competed in both local and general elections, obtaining significant results. As for myself, I decided not to bow out : I would be a candidate in the 1992 presidential election. Whatever happened, I refused to "tiptoe" away from my responsibilities. I had no illusions, but still insisted on standing. When I took third place behind Lissouba and Kolelas[1], this left me in a position to determine the result. I chose to support Lissouba.

— *Why that choice ?*

I thought Lissouba was more experienced than Kolelas. He knew what government was all about, having served as a Minister for a long time and as

---

1. Bernard Kolelas, President of the Congolese Movement for Democracy and Integral Development (MCDDI), an influential political party at the National Conference.

Prime Minister too. So on the basis of an agreement on government between his party and mine, I offered him my support. As you know, I carried out my duty, ensuring that power was transferred democratically in conditions of peace and security.

– 6 –

RETREAT TO OYO

Betrayal – The retreat – Civil war – A scattered opposition

— *So Pascal Lissouba was elected President in the second round of voting, but then decided not to honour the agreement made with you.*

Yes. It says a great deal about his attitude towards democracy. Yet to be frank, I still don't know why he did it ! In any case, my party chose to form an alliance with Kolelas's at that point, which changed the majority in Parliament. Since the Constitution adopted at the National Conference stated that the parliamentary majority would form the government, the country found itself in a delicate position. Barely three months after his election, the Head of State no longer had a majority to govern ! Remembering the difficulties that France, a longstanding democracy, faced during the first and second periods of an opposition parliamentary majority under President François

Mitterrand, did we have the option and means to manage this democratic crisis, an unprecedented, premature one for the Congo ?

In any case, President Lissouba refused to appoint a Prime Minister from the parliamentary majority and instead decided to dissolve the Assembly, which it was in his power to do. Following a protest demonstration organised by the opposition in front of the French Cultural Centre in Brazzaville, militiamen recruited by Lissouba – who no longer trusted the army – fired on the crowd, killing three people and wounding around ten. Subsequently, a government of national union was formed, but at what a price !

– *What did you decide at that point ?*

I was facing increasingly frequent attempts to upset and bully me on the part of the regime in power, which seemed afraid of me. Rather than react and run the risk of endangering our young democracy, I decided to withdraw to Oyo. This was in November 1992. Since the President feared me, I thought it best to leave and give him no excuse to blame me for his own inconsistencies, incompetence and erratic ways, and especially deny him any perceived provocation that could lead to an incident.

– *What happened while you were in Oyo ?*

An early general election was organised in May and June 1993. Given the balance of power at that point, the voting could only go against Lissouba. During the night, when the Minister of the Interior began to announce obviously falsified results, Kolelas's angry partisans immediately took to the streets in protest. Lissouba ordered his forces to patrol the capital. The army entered the southern districts of Brazzaville and there were clashes. Three people died in the first few hours. Subsequently, the situation worsened, degenerating into civil war. This was the hour of the militias : Lissouba's against Kolelas's, the worst of scenarios. Around thirty were killed.

— Was the rather questionable handling of the elections the only reason for this outbreak of violence ?

No. There was also the fact that Lissouba had been selling off the country's wealth at bargain prices in a frantic effort to raise enough funds to snatch a victory, and news of this got out.

— What had he done ?

He'd made a deal with the American oil company Oxy, selling the production of the N'Kossa oilfield at the ludicrous price of two or three dollars a barrel, instead of the normal twelve or thirteen ! In return, Oxy put money into the State coffers so Lissouba could pay the outstanding salaries of civil servants in an attempt to ensure voter loyalty. When details of the agreement came out, it drew very strong criticism from Elf, Oxy's direct competitor.

— A tough question : do you think that despite its horrors, civil war might ultimately be an inevitable precursor of democracy ? There are plenty of examples of this in the history of Europe, not to mention the United States.

Someone actually did suggest that during the violence in the Congo. An inevitable precursor ? Yes, when there's a revolution, but at the time, we didn't need an insurrection to achieve a multiparty system since it was accepted by everyone. When there's premature commitment to a process, before the people are ready for it – for democracy isn't plain sailing – can it be said that civil war is the price to pay to see it through to the end ? I don't think that's the right question. Today, the question we should perhaps be asking ourselves is whether the violence genuinely advanced the cause of democracy. I don't think it did, because in countries such as ours, violence of that kind aggravates divisions and differences, widening rifts and leading to resentment. These divisions – especially ethnic ones – are already awkward enough to handle ordinarily, there's really no need to aggravate them. In any case, there's no guarantee whatsoever that democracy will follow revolutionary violence.

Look at what happened in France, where the 1789 revolution led to the Empire.

— So for you, this civil war only aggravated the country's ethnic divisions ?

Well, the fact is that it didn't further democracy !
Ethnic divisions have been at the heart of the different civil wars in the Congo. To simplify, we could say that the 1993-1994 clashes were between natives of Pool – Kolelas's region – and the Niari Valley – pro-Lissouba. Later, during the fighting between my partisans and Lissouba's in 1997, the clashes tended to be north-south, although it wasn't as clear-cut as that. In the end, though, the violence solved nothing. On the contrary. That's why I'm very cautious about the question of such excesses being an inevitable precursor of democracy.

— Why are there so many political parties in the Congo – more than a hundred ? Is it due to tradition, the content of the political debate or perhaps the nature of the Congolese themselves ?

It isn't tradition, no. If we look at the situation in our country in the days of independence in the early Sixties, there were three political parties. All were all present throughout the country, although their leaders may sometimes have seemed to repre-sent only part of the country, a limited number of ethnic groups or a dominant ethnic group.

However, there was still a slight ideological divide, you might call it. Some identified with the SFIO, the French Socialists ; others with the French right. My feeling is that the situation was a little healthier. The political debate was more open and based on ideas and manifestos. Today's proliferation of parties doesn't improve the democratic debate, it confuses and even obscures issues, muddying the waters. So why all these parties ? In my view, the answer is often either ambition, determination to exist at any cost or pork-barrel politics. A given leader may plan on gaining a small degree of recognition or some kind of success as a politician. It may provide material for a certain number of discussions, but I can't really see why the three and a half million inhabitants of our country need nearly a hundred and fifty political parties to express themselves !

— *The question is all the more pertinent since many of these political movements are in opposition. To make their voice heard, they'd do better to merge or at least form a group. Their lack of unity doesn't work in their favour at all.*

True. To illustrate that, at the opposition's last conference, its leaders failed to agree on a joint candidate to stand against the ruling group we represent today in the next presidential election[1].

---

1. In July 2009.

— But wouldn't you like to have an opposition to engage in dialogue... as well as to cross blades with, of course ?

I'm not saying I have no political leaders to work with. There are many of them in the Congo, most of whom have actually served as my Prime Ministers or Ministers. Today, they're candidates for the office of President. Do these personalities represent genuine organised political forces, though ? That's very much the question. We should give them time. In fact, to enable the emergence of a true, nationally representative opposition able to enhance the political debate in this country, we are reviving the law that provided for the formation of political parties on a multiethnic basis — true parties on a national scale, which would be funded by the State. We think that's the best option to explore. Ultimately, it will mean the Congo has three or four major parties led by strong personalities, with clear policies and choices to offer the people, engaging in that healthy, open form of debate that is valuable — indeed vital — to any democracy.

— When is it due to come into force ?

I hope it will be passed by the end of 2009. Then the different movements and splinter groups will be able to get together if they so wish and form more solid parties in accordance with the law.

THE POLITICAL WILDERNESS

Transfer of power – Oyo –
The mango tree, the river and the mouse –
Exile in Paris – Preparing to return

– Would you explain why you decided to withdraw temporarily from political life in 1992 and return to your roots in Oyo ?

Actually, I only remained in my native region for a few months. I travelled to France in December, then finally returned to Oyo in April 1993 to take part in an early general election. I stayed there until July 1995. When I left Brazzaville, the situation in the country was already beginning to deteriorate alarmingly. I wanted to get away from that zone of instability, but mainly I was determined to avoid giving President Lissouba an excuse to try anything that might trigger a tragedy. In fact, I felt Lissouba was ill at ease while I was there. Although I'd supported him in his election, he was uncomfortable with my presence in Brazzaville. I believe he was unhappy about it right from the 31st August 1992, the day when I handed over power. On that day, when I left the Presidential Palace after the ceremony to make my way home, I was escorted and cheered all along the way by a vast crowd. I'd lost the election and a new President had been chosen, but he was almost alone in the Palace for his inauguration party, while I, his unfortunate opponent, was given such a send-off by the people who followed me when I left the Palace that they danced round my house all night ! As you can imagine, that was enough to upset President Lissouba. Then I felt that with the dissolution of Parliament and the increase in tension between the partisans of Lissouba and Kolelas, the situation might well become increasingly difficult and even dangerous for me in Brazzaville, so it would be better if I stepped back from the problem and withdrew to Oyo.

– But you carried on seeing people ?

I wanted to get away to think things over – my party continued to function normally – but I didn't want to think on my own. Many leaders and officials came to see me in Oyo to review the situation in the country and analyse the alarming consequences of the National Conference. Our discussions were very constructive. We talked for long hours under the mango trees by the river.

I took a lot of notes during these discussions. The question that came up all the time was how to get out of the blind alley we were in. Obviously, our position could have been worse. After all, there was a president and a government running the country. Even so, the Congo had been sucked dry and violence was flaring up time and again. The "gap years" continued in teaching, civil servants' salaries weren't paid for long stretches and things were no better in the private sector. I think it was then that those in positions of responsibility began to have doubts and came in increasing numbers to see me in Oyo. I won't say they'd begun to think, "Were we right to let President Sassou go ?", but in any case, they seemed genuinely interested in what I might have to say. I valued those long discussions and greatly enjoyed welcoming those people during my two years in Oyo.

– *What was your life like at the time ?*

It wasn't easy. Oyo was a village with no water mains or electricity. I had a generator, but it needed fuel to run on, which wasn't always available. And if there was no electricity, there was no water either, because there was no power to run the pump ! In these rather Spartan conditions, I began to sort out my notes and work on the political programme presented in my book *Le Manguier, le fleuve et la souris (The mango tree, the river and the mouse)* [1].

---

1. Published in French by Éditions Jean-Claude Lattès, Paris, 1997.

— Why that title ?

The mango tree because, as I mentioned, many of the discussions I had with my fellow citizens took place beneath such a tree. The river because we were sitting by the Alima, the river that runs beside my house in Oyo. The mouse is a little more complicated to explain. When I was President of the Republic, I gave one of my closest associates responsibility for the trade-union movement. He was a man I trusted completely and who seemed loyal to me. So loyal, in fact, that on one occasion, looking very determined, he told me : "President, if anything serious should happen, if your opponents want to walk over you, they'll have to walk over me first !" Well, it was this individual who led the unions in a general strike, paralysing the country and implicitly encouraging the political forces that were in favour of insurrection to take part in the movement. One day, I told that story to a few elders who were gathered under the mango tree. I was describing my shock at this close associate's betrayal, when one of them smiled and asked me, "How can you ask a question like that ? Don't you know our saying ? The mouse that nibbles our heel during the night always comes out from under our own bed." That's why the mouse features in the title of my book.

— During your time in Oyo, since you knew your successor might be uneasy about you, did you ever fear for your life ? Did you think an "accident" might happen ?

Yes, I did. The authorities actually had nine "checkpoint" roadblocks between Brazzaville and Oyo. The most dangerous was a hundred kilometres away. It was manned by troops sent from the capital – a company of soldiers, I think – who caused a lot of problems. Almost every day, there was an incident at one of the checkpoints with one or another of my many visitors. I thought a tragedy might eventually occur, which is why I decided to leave the Congo temporarily for Paris, to avoid any incident following some act of provocation.

— Did you stay in your house in Le Vésinet ?

No, the house in Le Vésinet was uninhabitable. It was an old house in very poor condition. I stayed in my apartment on the Avenue Rapp. I only went to Le Vésinet to work on my new book and to get away and enjoy the little garden in summer.

— How long did you stay in Paris and what did you live on ?

I stayed in Paris for nearly two years. My financial resources were those of a former President of the Republic.

— What did you do in Paris ? Did you maintain your contacts ?

Actually, for those two years, I wasn't politically active in the proper sense. I didn't meet with the press and I didn't give any interviews.

— Why such a determined silence ?

Because at that time, I'd decided to work on my political programme. I'd actually decided to stand in the next presidential election.

— Did you continue to meet your fellow citizens ?

Yes. It was a little more difficult for them, because officials who remained close to me were also in the "political wilderness" and it wasn't easy for them to afford a flight to Paris. Some managed the trip, though, and I enjoyed talking to them.

— When someone has been in power like you, when they have been so involved in the life of their country, how do they feel about these periods away from public life ?

I was naturally anxious about the situation in my country. I decided to ask certain foreign political leaders of my acquaintance for their assessment of it. I wrote to President Chirac and Bill Clinton, then I went to Cape Town to see President Mandela, a personal friend. Our private conversation over lunch lasted for hours, with only an inter-preter present. I asked President Mandela if he would intervene to ensure that calm, peaceful, democratic elections would be held at the end of President Lissouba's term of office. He agreed to this mediation role. As soon as I returned to Paris, his ambassador brought me a copy of the letter he'd immediately sent to Lissouba. Lissouba rejected his offer of mediation.

All through 1996, I visited different African countries. I met Presidents Bongo of Gabon, Biya of Cameroon, Déby of Chad, Bédié of Ivory Coast, Rawlings of Ghana, Kérékou of Benin, Diouf of Senegal, Compaoré of Burkina Faso, Dos Santos of Angola and Chissano of Mozambique. They all welcomed me warmly. I didn't ask any of them for their support, but simply drew their attention to the prevailing situation in the Congo, which I felt had the potential for great danger. I wanted them to use their influence with the Brazzaville autho-rities to make sure the coming presidential election would be organised democratically.

— Did these different meetings leave you feeling vindi-cated, or did the Heads of State try to convince you not to stand again, telling you, "Let it go"?

Oh no, not at all ! There was no question of that ! In any case, I didn't ask for their opinion on whether or not I should stand again in the presi-dential election. In fact, they were all sorry to see my country getting into worse difficulties and some of them acknowledged that the Congo hadn't fared too badly when I was Head of State. I must say that more and more Congolese were thinking the same. I'm not saying they were all sorry I'd gone, but they were starting to think that things were actually better before. I was receiving increasing numbers of messages from my fellow citizens of every walk of life and station asking me to come back. They all encouraged me to step into the electoral fray.

– 8 –

READY ONCE AGAIN

Back in Brazzaville – More betrayals
– Civil war again – On the principle
of democracy

– So you returned to the Congo in January 1997.

I returned on the 26th January 1997.

– And this time, you didn't stay in Oyo.

No, I moved back to Brazzaville. In fact, my
return to the capital caused quite a stir. Everything
came to a stop when I arrived. The people were
in the street, celebrating. President Lissouba left
the city to avoid having to hear about it. It took
me four hours to travel by car from the airport to
my house in M'Pila ! I was with Professor Claude
Maylin, a French oncologist from the Saint-Louis
hospital in Paris, a man I'd met during my "wilderness years" who'd asked to accompany me. He
was the only European in our little group. When

we arrived in Brazzaville, certain people thought he was some kind of "mercenary" or "éminence grise", which we found very amusing. It was actually the first time he'd set foot in the Congo and the only link between us was the friendly relationship we'd established over the previous months ! As we struggled through a cheering crowd and reached a crossroads near the Presidential Palace, I remember Claude Maylin pointing at the building left empty by its occupant and suddenly joking : "So why don't you go straight there ?" I told him I wouldn't countenance seizing power by force and intended to abide by the verdict of universal suffrage.

A few days later, I was greeted just as enthusiastically in Pointe-Noire. This time it took me five hours to get to my villa from the airport through the cheering crowds. A very powerful movement was gathering momentum. This was confirmed during my tour of the three regions of the Centre-North : Plateaux, Cuvette and Cuvette-Ouest. I believe that President Lissouba was staggered and certainly alarmed by this enthusiasm, especially since the polls he's said to have commissioned from specialised French institutes – I don't have formal proof of this – predicted he would lose if a presidential election were organised in July 1997. So he had to find a way of extending his term of office and postponing the election until things looked better for him.

 — *It was at that point that the situation in the country began to deteriorate ?*

Absolutely. We should remember that an article of the 1992 Constitution stated that if a major incident were to occur during the election campaign or if a presidential candidate were to die, then the Head of State could take steps to delay the election, extending their term of office.

 — *Can you tell us exactly what happened ?*

There were incidents on my campaign tour, first in the three regions I mentioned, then in Owando, the administrative centre of the Cuvette region where I was born. I saw that as political malice on the part of President Lissouba. He was seeking incidents in my own native region ! The Owando incident was serious — fatal in fact. Conveniently for Lissouba, the investigation found that those involved had escaped to my residence in M'pila, Brazzaville. On the 5th June 1997 at around four or five in the morning, the army — yes, the army ! — arrived in armoured vehicles and took up position, surrounding the district where my house was located to detain these alleged fugitives. It was all quite outrageous ! The situation very soon grew strained and then broke down, pitting army and police forces against my partisans, who'd been on the alert since the incidents in Owando.

71

— *That was what triggered the second civil war.*

Lissouba intentionally caused the incident because he was afraid of losing the election.

— *What did you do then ?*

Politically, the issue was to survive. In any case, the decision wasn't mine alone, there were all my partisans who wouldn't consider giving in : they were determined to hold out. Things moved very quickly. In two days, the situation deteriorated dramatically, from the surrounding of my residence to pitched battles between my partisans on the one hand and army and police units under orders from the government on the other. The clashes were particularly violent. On the third or fourth day, seeking weapons, my partisans launched offensives against army barracks. They didn't meet with any real resistance.

— *Could you foresee what would happen, that this would dissolve into a new civil war that would devastate the country ?*

No. I didn't think it would be so serious. However, I was convinced we had to protect ourselves. Faced with a regime that had used constant intimidation and violence for five years, we also had to show our determination to put an end to this by democratic means. Things got out of hand on both sides.

— Did the conflict spread beyond the capital?

No, from June to October, it was essentially limited to Brazzaville. It was only later that it spread to other regions of the country. In the north, Lissouba decided to use a number of political allies against us, including the Prime Minister, Yhombi Opango, in order to control certain provincial administrative centres. Militarily, we couldn't accept that — we saw the northern zone as our rear base — and had to carry out individual operations in Owando and two or three other locations to bring them under our control. These weren't spectacular operations, though. They lasted two or three days and brought all the regions we felt were strategic for us at the time under the control of our partisans.

— So each movement had its home territory. In Brazzaville itself, there were quite clear demarcation lines. These partisans you mention, though, weren't they actually armed militia?

Armed militia, yes.

— Where did these militia come from? Were they the legacy of the people's militia founded during the Marxist-Leninist regime?

Not at all. If that were the case, Kolelas wouldn't have had any militia, but he did. When it decided to govern by force and flout the rules of democracy, Lissouba's regime was responsible for the formation of these groups. Personally, I had partisans and I had no need of militiamen, unlike Kolelas, who needed them very early on, in 1993. It was when they saw what was happening that my partisans decided to arm themselves as a precautionary measure.

— *How and by whom were these militia armed ?*

Many were armed by sympathisers, especially ethnic sympathisers in the armed forces themselves. Weapons left military camps and stores and were taken to the different districts. No political party had the means or outside support needed to acquire weapons. It was essentially equipment changing hands within the country that armed the militia.

— *You yourself received support from Angola ?*

A long time after, in October 1997.

— *How did you take the decision to appeal to Angola ? Was it when you felt you had to try and put a stop to this civil war ?*

It was not only that. It's important that people should know – too few are aware of this – that Lissouba was the political and even strategic ally of Jonas Savimbi, the leader of UNITA[1]. They were in direct contact. Savimbi was even officially welcomed in Brazzaville on our national holiday. Of course, the Congolese army uniforms were supplied by UNITA that year! A *de facto* strategic alliance had been concluded between Lissouba and Savimbi behind the back of the Angolan government. In fact, Lissouba received support from UNITA in the shape of both men and equipment. President Dos Santos refused to allow a regime supporting the rebel movement fighting him within his country to consolidate its hold to the north of its territory, so it was perfectly logical for the Angolan government to intervene against Lissouba's administration. Given that Lissouba also refused to participate in the Libreville negotiations organised by President Bongo and the UN mediator and attended by seven African heads of State, but preferred to go to Kinshasa and Kigali to seek military support there, it's obvious that the outcome could only be decided in the field.

---

1. The ethnically-based Angolan rebel movement, notably supported by apartheid-era South Africa.

– So you won with the military support of Angola. What lesson did you learn at the time ? It was a relief, of course, but it must be hard to win a civil war.

Yes, it was very hard ! Very, very hard. But the main thing was to make sure it ended rapidly. In other countries, civil wars of that kind had dragged on endlessly, claiming hundreds of thousands of lives and causing millions of civilian casualties. In Africa, Rwanda, Sudan, Ethiopia, and Eritrea among others were devastated by civil wars. Some states such as Somalia literally disintegrated and even ceased to exist.

– Do you think that the Congo was on the verge of breaking up at that moment ?

I don't think so, but it wasn't good for such a conflict to drag on. Not only was it claiming more and more victims, but it was impossible to say what form it might ultimately take.

– If we draw a comparison with Western democracies, France, Italy and Germany among others experienced this kind of division. Originally, they were simply a collection of small ethnic groups. It's taken them centuries to become what they are today. At the time of these upheavals, the Congo was very young. In fact, it's still a young country.

Yes, I won't say there was no risk. In a situation of this kind, you can never rule out the fragmentation hypothesis totally. But with the Congo, I don't think there was a possibility of a break-up on ethnic lines. In fact, no-one considered that outcome.

— So in October 1997, with help from Angola, you put an end to the civil war. You stopped the bloodbath in your country, but you used armed force to return to power.

How could we do otherwise to stop what you call a "bloodbath" ? We used force to intervene and dealt a powerful blow to make it all stop. There was absolutely no intention on my part to seize power by force, no intention to mount a coup ! I must stress that. Many people have got it wrong and still take a simplistic view of what happened. As I've already said, when I returned to the Congo, it was to stand in the presidential election – in other words, to abide by the rules of democracy. In fact, it was to ensure compliance with those rules that I contacted all the Heads of State I mentioned earlier during the year leading up to my return to Brazzaville, asking them to intervene in favour of scrupulously legal elections. If I'd been planning any kind of coup, I wouldn't have done what I did ! Then it should be remembered that after restoring confidence, security and peace in the country, I set the Congo back on the path of democracy – by reviving its institutions and organising elections – and development, by stabilising the economy, damaged by years of civil war.

— Generally, do you think that the concept of democracy reflects the same reality in Europe as in Africa, for instance ? In other words, is democracy universal, or must it be adapted to the specific identity of different countries ?

Democracy is the same for every country. The principle that the people choose their leader is a universal one. Although, having made that point, I think it would be incorrect to say that a people that has enjoyed democracy for two centuries is exactly the same as one that has had only five years of democratic life. Also, when a large part of a country's population is unable to read or write, I think it is hard to believe it will find it as easy to understand the democratic process, its issues and the different programmes presented by candidates as a country whose population is educated. We could discuss this question endlessly, but that's the reality. We can say there's only one form of democracy, but that it doesn't work in the same way everywhere given the different situations in different countries. That is why I've felt the need to move in stages in the Congo, although without losing sight of the final democratic goal.

— Could we say, for instance, that one of the characteristics of democracy in Africa is the importance of the leader, whose personality can help to unite a nation, perhaps more than in Europe ?

It's the same everywhere. We mentioned Italy and Germany earlier. At one point in their histories, those two European nations had leaders – Garibaldi in Italy and Bismarck in Germany – who brought unity to their countries and accelerated their historical development. Always and everywhere, there have been figures who leave their mark on the history of their country and sometimes the world. There are such people in Europe, in Africa and elsewhere.

– 9 –

TWELVE YEARS AS PRESIDENT :
A POLITICAL APPRAISAL

Getting the country moving again –
Congolese political life – The new generations

– In political terms, how would you assess these last twelve years as leader of the Congo, President ?

First, we must remember that when I returned to power in October 1997, the country was at a standstill, with no political institutions or administration. The educational system had been stalled for months and the capital was in ruins. So the priority was to get the State running once again, but the conditions weren't at all right for even starting things up again. So I organised a conference with different elements of the nation – representatives of the regions, political parties, associations and Congolese expatriates – to study the vital minimum to be accomplished over the next three years. Those three years were to be a transitional

81

period. In my opinion, that was a suitable length of time to revive the country.

Our conference resulted in a transitional parliament, elected during this gathering and made up of representatives of political parties and associations, members of civil society and leading personalities. A transitional government was also formed to implement a precise programme of national reconstruction. However – and I must stress this – our main objective was to restore the population's confidence, shaken by that terrible civil war. For us, the priority was to do all we could to ensure that the different communities of our Congo would all accept each other. We then organised a Convention, to which the political leaders in exile were invited.

– *Except Lissouba and Kolelas.*

Lissouba and Kolelas didn't come, but all the others made the journey. They took part in this Convention, whose objective was to lay down a certain number of rules with the aim of restoring peace and security throughout the country and reviving democratic political life, with a view to preparing the Congo for fresh elections. A number of immediate steps were taken. Unfortunately, they didn't prevent Lissouba's partisans in Dolisie in the Niari region and Kolelas's in the Pool region from launching new hostilities. Neither of the two men had come to Brazzaville to attend our reconciliation conference. They decided to remain abroad, but continued to stir up their partisans in the Congo from exile. We succeeded in restoring relative calm in the areas affected, enabling local, general and presidential elections to be held in 2002. So we moved on from the transitional period to a period that can be described as "normal", with a parliament and president elected by direct universal suffrage.

— *Lissouba and Kolelas's parties took part in these elections.*

Yes, but to a very minor extent. They actually had little influence on the population. The aim of the vast majority of the Congolese was to see peace, stability and security restored. I must confess that the election was quite easy for me. I understood what my fellow citizens were thinking : "President Sassou is the only personality who can bring stability to the country. We have to trust him." This was such a general feeling that I had no difficulty conducting my campaign in Lissouba's and Kolelas's traditional strongholds – in other words, among the populations of the south of the country, including the people of Pool. In fact, by that point, the inhabitants of the Pool region were so keen to find a personality who'd be able to restore peace that they elected me with a large majority. Several candidates understood this and joined me.

— Yet a pocket of resistance made up of Pastor Ntumi's partisans still remained in Pool.

We were able to hold the presidential election in Pool, but not the local and general elections, since the region was not sufficiently organised for voting to take place in all the constituencies. This meant that Pool was only able to return a few deputies to parliament.

— What's the situation in Pool today[1] ?

The problem has been solved. Ntumi has formed his party. Today, at the end of my term of office, I can say that peace, stability and security have been restored throughout the country.

— So you feel you've honoured your commitments in political terms ?

The different institutions worked normally throughout the period and elections were held democratically at set dates.

— Speaking of the electoral process, a commission was appointed to make sure the next presidential election goes smoothly in July 2009. Can you guarantee its impartiality ?

---

1. May 2009.

The commission is made up of representatives of the majority parties, the opposition parties and civil society. It's chaired by a neutral personality : a judge. I should point out that judges cannot join political parties in the Congo.

— *So no-one can challenge the work of this commission ?*

In principle, no.

— *The Congolese refrained from voting in the last local elections. There was a high rate of abstention. How do you explain this disaffection ? Is it due to the political situation, the splintered state of the parties or the difficulties electors have in making sense of things ? Or is it perhaps due to a lack of interest in local politics, as has been the case elsewhere ?*

No, I don't think voters are losing interest in local and regional affairs – at least, not in the Congo – even though we did see a surprising rate of abstention in the last elections. I think it was due to genuine dysfunctions in the practical organisation of the elections, IT dysfunctions that led to problems with the electoral rolls : voters not registered or registered twice, the wrong polling stations listed, and so on. That was a genuine problem, especially in the general election. These mistakes were later corrected, so more people voted in the local elections, even though the local elections with their lists of candidates – which really are quite daunting – don't generally attract large numbers of voters. People prefer to vote for a candidate they're familiar with, a candidate whose programme they know, as in the general and presidential elections, rather than a list made up of relatively unfamiliar names. This is especially true of our fellow citizens who can't read or write and have trouble with a list-based election. However, I'm convinced that if the preliminary work currently being done before the presidential election of July 2009 is successful, the abstention rate should be lower than in the general and local elections, even if certain social problems and unsatisfied demands on the right and left may lead some voters to lose interest in the election for various reasons. In any case, the technical problems observed during previous elections – which in my opinion go a long way towards explaining the abstention rate – seem to have been solved.

– *Is there new blood in the Congo political class? Are young people coming forward who are interested in running the country?*

Yes, in quite large numbers. Many political parties are formed by young people. We sense there's a surge. Among women, too. In fact, we're helping them to play a greater role and take more of an interest in public affairs. However, the quality of the young men and women entering the field of politics is another matter. While there are increasing numbers of young people who wish to play a part in public life and form parties, and who hope to help run the country tomorrow, how many are ready to take on political responsibilities today ? No-one can say. You know, in politics, the road is long and littered with obstacles. It requires a great deal of self-denial, sacrifice and hard work. You really have to believe in it. However, I'm sure that the Congo has no lack of young people who'll be able to take over one day.

— *Are the elders making way for younger people ?*

Certainly. Those of our political leaders who can be viewed as elders are beginning to take their leave : Kolelas, Yhombi, Lissouba and others. In fact, at 66 or 67, I'm beginning to think about my departure myself, since our Constitution specifies that no-one over 70 can stand in the presidential election.

— *Does that mean that if you're re-elected in July 2009, it will be your last term of office ?*

Well, in any case, the Constitution stipulates that the president can't serve more than two terms.

TWELVE YEARS AS PRESIDENT :
AN ECONOMIC APPRAISAL

Reconstruction – Water – Electricity
– Migration to the Cities

— Perhaps we can move on to an economic appraisal of your last twelve years in office, President. Are you generally satisfied ?

Well, it's not all good news, but then that's the case virtually everywhere ! A full-on economic crisis has engulfed the world without warning. Even so, there's been some remarkable progress over the last twelve years in our country. Remember that when we returned to power, the country was at a total economic standstill. For example, both the port of Pointe-Noire and the Brazzaville-Pointe-Noire railway were out of service, making it almost impossible to keep the economy going. Ships could no longer enter the port of Pointe-Noire because it was completely silted up, so the first urgent step I took was to bring in

dredging equipment to deepen the water sufficiently – to twelve metres at least – for the port
to operate, restoring it to its former role as one of
the main deep-water ports on the Atlantic Coast
of Africa.

The second decision was to reconstruct six
bridges on the Brazzaville-Pointe-Noire railway
line, which had been damaged or destroyed during
the civil war, preventing any trains from running.
For two years, from 1998 to 2000, freight had to
be airlifted between Brazzaville and Pointe-Noire !
Meanwhile, we had to get all the administrative
departments – such as finance and customs and
revenue – back into working order and put the
banking system back on its feet.

– To do that, you went to the IMF ?

Yes, there were high-level negotiations with the
international financial institutions, the International Monetary Fund and the World Bank. The
State had to privatise the banks and take over their
debt. We restored stability to the entire system in
that way, before setting up new banks. Today, we
can say that the banking sector of our economy is
working perfectly. There is even some overliqui-
dity. Since we overhauled the system, new banks
have come to the Congo. Accreditation applica-
tions are currently being examined.

To stimulate consumer demand in the country,
money had to start circulating again, meaning that

wages had to be paid. Civil servants hadn't received their salaries for fourteen or fifteen months ! So we had to find the money for the months to come at least, even if we couldn't pay the arrears. In the cities, almost all the shops had been destroyed and there were no longer any markets. We had to sort all that out.

— You did have oil revenue, though.

Yes, but don't forget that oil was only nine dollars a barrel at the time. This was in 1997-1999 and oil prices have shot up since then. Also, during the civil war, Lissouba had transferred the State Treasury to the southern district of Brazzaville and it had vanished without trace. So there was no more Treasury, which essentially consisted of oil revenue. The Congolese State had no reserves. Even the Treasury building was in ruins. So working with the international institutions, we launched an emergency programme that gradually enabled us to get the State running again, pay civil servants regularly and restore the trust of our partners, both inside and outside the country.

— Did the IMF do all you'd hoped or did you have to rely on other sources ?

The International Monetary Fund doesn't have money to lend to States unless they comply with a set of performance criteria. If you're unable to repay a debt and the experts feel your administrative, economic and financial organisation isn't sufficiently efficient or your management open enough, the IMF has no money to lend you. So we had to negotiate agreements with the Fund to satisfy a certain number of performance criteria. Working with the IMF and the World Bank, we entered the "Heavily-Indebted Poor Countries Programme" to reschedule our debt with our different creditors and even have part of it cancelled. We're still applying that programme today.

As time went by, the Congo achieved significant successes on an economic level, especially thanks to renewed activity in the oil and logging sectors. In the logging sector, we made decisions that led to nearly 80 % of wood being transformed nationally, creating many jobs.

As for the education system, after two "gap years", it was at a standstill and had to be reorganised. Today, although the general level has declined and there are still problems with facilities, especially in the interior of the country, and even if there aren't yet enough teachers, we note with satisfaction that the "machine" is up and running again. Examinations are held regularly from primary-school to university level. Our country is once again a nation with a very high rate of school attendance.

– For years, two recurrent problems have handicapped the Congo : water and electricity supply. What's the situation today ?

The public-utility issues we face in the cities, Brazzaville and Pointe-Noire, are due to the production system. For a long time, we relied on the Inga dam on the Congo River in the Democratic Republic of the Congo [1], and during my previous term of office, we planned a high-tension line linking Inga to Brazzaville. However, due to its poor performance, the Inga dam can't satisfy the needs of Brazzaville. In fact, it can't even supply enough power for Kinshasa !

I'm aware that our electricity production is insufficient at present. The Moukoukoulou dam in Bouenza supplies 74 megawatts, the Djoué dam in Brazzaville 15 megawatts and the gas-fired power station in Pointe-Noire 22 megawatts, a total of 111 megawatts for the whole country, which is nothing ! Since we can't supply what we don't have, we've had to make some very important decisions. With Chinese co-operation, we've started work on a 120-megawatt hydroelectric dam in Imboulou on the Léfini river, two hundred kilometres to the north of Brazzaville, which I think will be generating its first megawatts by the end

---

1. Democratic Republic of the Congo (DRC), formerly the Belgian Congo and subsequently Zaire. To the east and south of the Republic of the Congo.

of the year. We've also decided to build a 30-mega-watt oil-fired power station in Brazzaville and a 300-megawatt gas-fired power station in Pointe-Noire in partnership with an Italian company, ENI. Then we have generators more or less all through the interior of the country. They're obviously not an ideal solution since they use a lot of fuel, but our electricity problem will only be solved if we complete the production programme we've planned. It's a major programme and it will be a while before it's implemented and begins to have an appreciable effect.

The same is true of the water supply. We've laun-ched programmes to double the volume of the water supply, but the water problem is closely linked to the issue of electricity – the pumps are electric. We're implementing a programme to double water production in Brazzaville and Pointe-Noire as part of what we call "accelerated muni-cipalisation". In a word, we should achieve the first perceptible results in relation to electricity and water supply very soon.

— *When you say "very soon" that means by... ?*

By 2010 at the latest.

— *Looking at farming, there's a severe problem in this sector : only 2 % of Congolese land is farmed today.*

That's true. Farming is a challenge that we genuinely need to deal with. We already have a food security programme, we've set up an agricultural fund and we've also developed a mechanisation programme. It will be one of the priority initiatives that we hope to launch over the next few years.

   — Following mass migration to the cities, the problem is to persuade the Congolese to go back and work on the land.

Yes. We can't ask them to farm the land by hand in the old way. Even if we did, they'd refuse. No, if we want to convince our young people to go back to work on the land, we have to offer them better conditions. That means training programmes, as well as farm mechanisation. It's quite a challenge, especially in terms of occupational training, and we plan to tackle it over the years to come. Our goals include training young people to enable them to obtain qualifications and providing them with jobs in different sectors of production, including farming.

– 11 –

THE CONGO AND THE WORLD ECONOMIC CRISIS

The crunch – Africa without a voice – The Chinese ally

– Over the last few months, the world has been hit by a financial and economic crisis that's fairly unprecedented in its ferocity. How is a country like the Congo affected by the phenomenon ?

Beyond simply managing the consequences of the crisis, which has hit the Congo as hard as it has any other country, this is certainly an opportunity to take a serious look at what capitalism means in our developing nations. Here, we can say that we don't have national capitalism as such, since whole sectors of our economy aren't controlled by the Congolese upper middle class. In the capitalist world, our countries have an outward-oriented economy. They're still completely dependent on outside influences and those outside influences don't necessarily have our development at heart !

— *How can you explain Africa's difficulty in making its voice heard at such important economic summits as the G20 ?*

The world is governed by power relationships. Africa – unfortunately, this is still the case today – continues to be seen as superfluous. No or little attention is paid to our continent at these international meetings. It has little economic, financial or military might, and since the disappearance of the two Cold-War blocs, it's no longer vital in geostrategic terms. Africa's actually a pool of raw materials and that's mainly how it's seen. Purely by chance, I saw a few African faces at the last G20 summit in London[1] on television. There was a representative of South Africa, and also the President of Ethiopia. Was he invited to the G20 to represent Africa ? Had he come to represent Africa ? I have no idea, but what influence can Ethiopia bring to bear on global decisions ? You see, when this sort of thing is done, it can have unforeseen consequences. In this case, it really seemed like a terrible caricature !

---

1. In April 2009.

— But wasn't there any collective approach from the African Union before the last G20 summit in London ?

The issue was raised in October 2008 at the meeting of French-speaking countries in Quebec, just a few days before President Sarkozy of France met President Bush. It was clearly agreed that the world stood at a crossroads and that there had to be a genuine, meaningful, worldwide discussion on how the international financial system could be reformed, taking the economic repercussions of the crisis into consideration. This was the position we all decided on at the French-speaking summit in Quebec and President Sarkozy was in agreement. Yet it seems his visit to Washington led to different choices. The African Union gave its opinion and the African Development Bank held a meeting of all the continent's Ministers of Finance and presented its conclusions. Apparently, they weren't taken into account.

— What concrete effects is the global crisis having on the Congo ?

The financial crisis has had a rapid impact on the economies of every country, but in developing nations such as ours, the impact's been immediate, because when the countries that import raw materials reduce or halt their industrial activity, we suppliers suffer the inevitable consequences. As you know, the fall in the price of oil, our main source of wealth, led to an aftershock. It dropped from 150 dollars a barrel to under 40. In just five or six months, we lost 100 dollars a barrel ! And that loss will directly impact on our development, as you can imagine. The logging sector, which was flourishing in the Congo a short time ago, is at a virtual standstill today. No-one wants to buy timber. If you go to the port of Pointe-Noire, you'll see mountains of unsold wood. Our government's been forced to introduce special measures to assist the logging sector. Then of course the economic crisis has aggravated the food crisis that affects most developing nations. We've had to take steps to manage this situation, providing relief for the most vulnerable social strata to enable them to survive.

— *I suppose all these measures taken together have had a serious effect on the economic life of the Congo.*

Yes, even when we planned the national budget for 2009 we had to draw up at least four successive versions ! Each time we finalised a draft, the price of oil fell and we had to start all over again. For instance, we prepared a budget based on a barrel of oil at $100, only to learn that the price of the barrel had dropped to $80 once the draft was finished. So we based new calculations on that figure, but by the time our work was done, the price of the barrel had plunged again to $60. And so on. Finally, we completed our budget proposal for 2009 just two months ago [1]. It wasn't at all easy. We also had to revise the country's growth forecasts each time. In the euphoria of a spectacular, sharp, substantial increase in the price of oil, all the analysts – including those at the International Monetary Fund, the World Bank and the Bank of Central African States – predicted that the Congolese economy would enjoy two-figure growth in 2009. We've had to scale that down and have now decided on a figure of 9 % – still a significant rate of growth – although it may be less. In any case, even if it's 8 %, 7 % or 6 %, we'll still be able to keep our head above water. The objectives of certain programmes already in progress have been revised downwards slightly and we haven't launched any new projects.

– Have you been forced to cut back on certain infrastructure programmes ? I'm thinking of the railway and the road networks.

We've done all we can to carry on with those programmes we'vealready begun, but we've no intention of starting up any more because today we no longer have the resources. Negotiations are continuing with our partners – especially the Bolloré group – to improve the rail system, though. Indeed, improving the performance of the Braz-

---

1. In March 2009.

zaville-Pointe-Noire rail link is vital for the activity
of the port of Pointe-Noire. For road infrastructure, we've secured credit at concessionary rates
from China. With the deferment that's been
granted, we believe the credit should be sufficient
to continue building the Pointe-Noire-Brazzaville,
Owando-Makoua-Ouesso, and Obouya-Boundji-
Gabon-border highways.

*– How would you describe your co-operation with
China ?*

Our co-operation with China is a win-win relationship. China needs raw materials and is also looking for sales outlets to sell its products. On our
side, we have tremendous financial and technical
needs if we're to build infrastructure and strengthen the foundations of our development. The
basis of the deal is very clear on both sides, which
is why I call it a win-win relationship. While some
specific agreements may benefit one partner more
than the other, it should balance out over our trade
as a whole. In any case, it will no longer be the
kind of unilateral relationship where Africa serves
as an outlet for products manufactured in China
and the Chinese come here to take Africans' jobs.
China isn't actually our only partner. Many African
countries are forging increasingly close economic
and trade relationships with India.

— *The Congo and China have particularly long-standing relations.*

Absolutely. We established diplomatic relations with the People's Republic of China in February 1964. In July of that year, I played a modest part in the very first Congolese delegation to visit China. There was a parliamentary deputy, a trade unionist, a leader of a women's organisation, a painter and an army officer – me. It wasn't easy to travel to China in those days. Leaving from Brazzaville, we had to go via Paris, Zurich, Cairo, Karachi, Dacca and Shanghai before we finally reached Beijing !

— *Didn't you meet Mao Zedong on that trip ?*

Our delegation was received by Mao and Zhou Enlai too. I've been back to China at least ten times since. So we have a long-established relationship with China and the Chinese and they're well aware of that. In 1964, there were perhaps only half a dozen African countries that recognised China – Nasser's Egypt, Ben Bella's Algeria, Sékou Touré's Guinea, Nkrumah's Ghana, Modibo Keita's Mali and the Congo. We've always maintained those relations, during both the Cold War and the Sino-Soviet split, which wasn't easy at times.

— China even aided UNITA at one point during the Angolan civil war, I believe.

Yes, while we Congolese supported the opposite side, the MPLA, as did the Soviets. Of course, when the Soviets were committed somewhere, the Chinese automatically joined the opposing faction. They even supported Mobutu! We had the same situation in Zimbabwe, with the two liberation movements, ZANU and ZAPU.

— But what could little Congo offer huge China at the time ?

Support at the United Nations. At the time, China wanted to be recognised and be able to sit as a permanent member of the Security Council in place of Taiwan. To end this chapter, let me tell you a story. One day in 1987 when I was President of the OAU and had toured almost the entire world to plead the cause of Southern Africa, I met Deng Xiaoping in Beijing. He was very old and ill. After assuring me that we naturally had China's support in our struggle to eradicate apartheid, he told me the story of the reforms he was introducing in his country, and added : "If the reforms I've begun continue at the same pace, if China's not fourth in the world by 2025, then it will be fifth, but certainly not sixth !" 2025 is still some way off, but you can draw your own conclusions.

China's become a major economic and commercial power. It's succeeding brilliantly in making the difficult transition from communism to the market economy.

– SECOND PART –

LOOKING BACK ON COLONISATION

— What's your opinion of the colonisation of Africa by different European powers : France, Britain, Portugal and Belgium ? Was it all the same or do you feel there were subtle distinctions or even clearer differences ?

I think there were a few subtle distinctions, although I'd like to stress that the principle of colonisation is always the same and obviously totally reprehensible in every way.

The principle of Portuguese colonisation was assimilation, so much so that many Africans in the territories concerned had to give up their names and use Portuguese ones, and certain towns had their names changed. Huambo became Nova Lisboa and Maputo Lourenço-Marques. Guinea-Bissau, the Cape Verde islands, Angola and Mozambique were considered part of Portugal. The colonisers who lived there acted as if they were their home, their country, and expressed the intention of developing them by building infrastructure, industry, and so on. They brought over large numbers of people from Portugal to work in all sectors of the economy to the detriment of the local populations, who were given no training. In the days of the Cuban presence in Angola during the civil war, Raul Castro, who was then Cuba's Minister of Defence, told me he'd had to put some of his soldiers to work as bus drivers because there weren't enough trained Angolans. In fact, through assimilation, the Portuguese intended to build settlements, rather like France in Algeria.

— That may have been why Africa's liberation struggles were more violent in countries colonised by the Portuguese. Moving on from Portugal, we come to the United Kingdom. What's your view of British colonisation ?

The British had rather different colonial policies. To begin with, unlike the Portuguese, they trained local elites.

— And French colonisation ?

France didn't greatly bother about developing the areas it occupied. You can see this by looking at the cities. Simply compare the cities developed by the Portuguese — Luanda, Nova Lisboa, Lourenço-Marques — which have economic activities, small and medium-sized businesses, processing industries and so on — to the cities left by French colonisation. Compare Libreville in 1960 — in the days of independence – with Luanda : they were like chalk and cheese ! The same goes for N'Djamena or Bangui. Even Brazzaville, the capital of French Equatorial Africa, was like a large market town.

– *You're hard on the French !*

Take the Congo. Today, nothing remains from the French colonial period in any part of my country except Brazzaville and Pointe-Noire. When the French colonists decided to occupy a particular part of the Congo, they only set up the basic resources needed to ship out local production, which was all sent to Metropolitan France.

– *That was the major companies.*

That was the major concessionary companies. They used the rivers to ship out raw materials or farm produce without building any infrastructure. I grew up next to a river, the Alima. Until independence, there was no port anywhere along the river, even though boats called at several different places to trade.

– *You feel it was total exploitation.*

Absolutely. Look at the construction of the railway from Brazzaville to the port of Pointe-Noire, essentially to ship out entire cargos of our

111

country's wealth to France. The *Congo-Océan* line was built with forced labour, costing nearly thirty thousand Congolese lives !

— *Finally, other colonists, the Belgians.*

Was that really colonisation ? That's a valid question, since today's Democratic Republic of the Congo was the exclusive property of King Leopold II. It was his personal possession !

– 13 –

WHY BRAZZAVILLE ?

An eventful visit to N'Djamena
– Sékou Touré's idea – A city
of powerful symbols

— While we're on the subject of colonisation, why is Braz-
zaville still called Brazzaville ? Why does the capital of the
Congo still bear the name of Pierre Savorgnan de Brazza[1] *?*

That's an issue we've discussed a number of
times in our country, especially during the Marxist-
Leninist revolution. Before I give my opinion, let
me tell you a little story. In 1979, the OAU had
just urgently requested that three countries send
interposition troops to Chad, where a civil war was
raging. Those countries were Sékou Touré's
Guinea, Mathieu Kérékou's Benin and the Congo.
In September, we met at the Non-Aligned Move-

---

1. Pierre Savorgnan de Brazza (1852-1905), a French
explorer of Italian extraction.

ment summit in Havana. The eldest among us, Sékou Touré, called Kérékou and me to his villa and explained : "The OAU's entrusted us with a mission. We have to send troops to take up position in Chad, between Goukouni Weddeye's and Hissène Habré's forces. What should we do ? We don't know what the situation is there !" He thought for a moment, then decided : "You, Sassou, you're the youngest. You can go as our scout and observe the situation in the field. You'll report back to us, then all three of us will go to N'Djamena."

So I left Havana on this mission. On the way, I asked the Secretary-General of the OAU, Edem Kodjo, and my Foreign Minister, Pierre Nzé, to join me. Off we went in a small plane lent by President Bongo, heading for N'Djamena. When we were directly above the Chadian capital, I looked down through the window at the ground and saw... nothing ! Visibly, no welcome had been organised for us – although I was young at the time, I was still President of the Republic and I was accompanied by two high-ranking political leaders. There was no guard of honour, no group of officials to be seen, not a single vehicle and not even a strip of red carpet ! We circled N'Djamena two or three times. Still nothing. What should we do ?

It was then that we saw a column of three or four Land Rovers arriving in a cloud of dust, packed with Toubou fighters armed to the teeth with sand-coloured scarves over their heads. This was hardly an improvement ! Who were these fighters ? What were they doing ? After thinking it over, I told the pilot to land. We would see what happened. Once we were on the ground, I saw a little man with an imposing head of hair climb down from one of the Land Rovers and hurry towards me : it was Goukouni Weddeye ! He embraced me and waved us into the cab of his vehicle. Inside, there were four or five of us and we could scarcely move. We raced through the city, sirens wailing and lights flashing, cannon in front of us, cannon behind us and cannon to the side of us. When we reached the Presidential Residence, we began talks immediately. I asked to speak to Colonel Kamougué too, the leader of Southern Chad. He was in his region when we contacted him and told us he would only come to N'Djamena if we could offer guarantees for his safety. "What guarantees ?" we asked him. He wanted a French Army helicopter. Not a problem. We called the French headquarters and secured their agreement. Soon, the helicopter was ready. Kamougué's next demand was that the Secretary General of the OAU and my Minister of Foreign Affairs should come and get him ! So Kodjo and Nzé climbed into the helicopter and went to fetch Kamougué, who then required the Secretary General of the OAU and the Minister of Foreign Affairs of the Congo to cross N'Djamena in the same vehicle as him. Finally, they brought Kamougué to me and discussions began, continuing until nightfall. That wasn't all, though :

the leader of Southern Chad insisted he should sleep in the same place as me, again for reasons of safety. The problem was that I didn't know where I was to sleep myself! No plans had been made. Finally, a villa was quickly prepared and we got through the night without mishap.

The next day, I took the still anxious Kamougué home. Back in Brazzaville, I contacted Sékou Touré and Kérékou to report on my mission. They decided to join me and all three of us went to N'Djamena. After studying the situation, we decided that each of our countries would send a battalion to Chad to form the interposition force requested by the OAU. However, in the end, only the Congo honoured its commitment. Neither Benin nor Guinea sent a single man. In Chad, our Congolese troops soon found themselves caught between the two factions, who'd begun to fight again. After losing three soldiers, I decided to evacuate our battalion from N'Djamena, where it was trapped. We were able to carry out this operation through Cameroon, via Kousseri, thanks to the good offices of President Ahidjo.

– *And Brazzaville ?*

I'm just getting to that! It was when we were heading back with Kérékou that Sékou Touré suddenly turned to me and said : "Listen, I haven't been to Brazzaville since 1963, "when he had come to Brazzaville and made an inflammatory speech that had helped to fire up the Congolese against their President of the day, Fulbert Youlou". I'll pay a quick visit to Mobutu in Kinshasa on the other side of the river and I'll be with you in the evening. Prepare a rally for me, I have to speak to the Congolese, a revolutionary people." I told him that wouldn't be a problem. It was very easy to mobilise the population during the Marxist-Leninist period.

So after visiting Mobutu, Sékou Touré returned to Brazzaville as planned at the end of the afternoon. Meeting him at the airport, I told him : "Elder, we're going to the rally. I'll introduce you and you can say what you have to say to the Congolese." "Oh," he answered, "I don't have much to say. I've just come to change the name of Brazzaville. I'm going to tell the Congolese that their capital will now be called Ngouabiville !" I was shocked ! "But elder, are you serious ?" "Of course I am," he answered, "that's why I asked you to organise a rally !" The conversation turned surrealistic.

"You won't do it ! I'm telling you, you won't do it !"

"Why not ? How can it be a problem for a revolutionary like you ?"

"I may be a revolutionary, but you won't do it !"

"Are you serious ?"

"Yes, very serious ! If the Congolese want to change the name of Brazzaville, that's their decision and our capital's name will change. If not, it's out of the question ! It's up to the people to decide !"

"You're really sure you don't want me to talk about a name change ?"

"You mustn't even try !"

The discussion lasted a good twenty minutes with the bemused Kérékou looking on. Then we went to the rally... where no-one mentioned a name change for Brazzaville !

— Perhaps we can come back to the question ?

Yes, I know, the story I've just told you was a little long, but hopefully, it provided you with a behind-the-scenes glimpse of what happens in the everyday lives of Heads of State. Stories of these occasions, which can be of varying importance, intensity or humour, are very rarely told, yet they can sometimes reveal a great deal or simply provide a better grasp of a situation, action or personality. Anyway, we haven't changed the name of Brazzaville because the Congolese have never wanted it changed ! Back then, some suggested it should be called Mfoa, which was the name of the village that grew into our capital, while others wanted to call it Ngouabiville as a tribute to the former President, but most preferred to keep the existing name. Of course, the founder of the city, Pierre Savorgnan de Brazza, was an explorer, not a coloniser. In fact, he was a humanist and fiercely opposed to the way in which the native population was treated, as shown by the many reports he sent to the French government. That's why we were happy to grant a request from Brazza's family – and it seems it was what Brazza himself wanted – for his ashes to be brought to the bank of the Congo river.

– And since the Second World War, Brazzaville had been a symbol of freedom for Africa.

Yes, because on the 26th October 1940, de Gaulle decreed that Brazzaville was the "capital of Free France". It was in Brazzaville that he founded the Order of the Liberation. It was also there that he made a famous speech on the 30th January 1944 recognising and proclaiming "the dignity and ability" of the peoples of Africa, a declaration that was immediately interpreted – especially by Africans – as a major political act, announcing an intention to set French Overseas Territories on the path of decolonisation. So as you can see, Brazzaville is a city loaded with history. It has its references – excellent references – and we have no reason to be ashamed of them, quite the contrary !

FRENCH PORTRAITS

The La Baule speech –
Hassan II's answer – The Dakar speech –
Remorse

– You're among the African Heads of State who've known the greatest number of French Presidents. I fully understand that your position forbids you from passing judgement on any of them, but taking them in chronological order, can you at least tell us how you saw them as both partners and individuals ?

I met President Giscard d'Estaing as soon as I came to power in 1979. It was in November of that year in Paris. I remember the official visit very well, because on the day I arrived in France, things were a little strained. The Minister of Labour, Robert Boulin, had just been found drowned in a pond not far from Paris. French newspapers were full of the event, of course. Despite this, my visit went very well. In fact, I had very little contact with President Giscard d'Estaing, but that didn't prevent relations between our two countries from being good during his seven-year term of office. Let's say he was more interested in other countries, such as Mobutu's Zaire, which was of greater strategic and economic importance to France in those days when the world was divided into two antagonistic blocs. Remember that French paratroopers were sent into Kolwezi, Katanga, in May 1978. President Giscard d'Estaing was also close to Houphouët-Boigny, I believe.

– Giscard d'Estaing was an ally of Mobutu and backed the FNLA[1] in the Angolan conflict.

Since he was close to the FNLA, that distanced him from us on the Angolan issue, since we supported the opposing movement, the MPLA[2].

– You knew François Mitterrand better.

Yes. Of course, he was President for longer too ! François Mitterrand made an official visit to the Congo. On that occasion, he awarded me the Grand-Croix de la Légion d'Honneur and I'm particularly proud of that. He and I achieved concrete results in terms of co-operation projects, such as

---

1. The National Front for the Liberation of Angola, backed especially by France and Mobutu's Zaire.
2. The Popular Movement for the Liberation of Angola, backed by the Soviet Union and Cuba.

the rehabilitation of the Brazzaville University Medical Centre, which required major funding, and, in quite another area, the formation of an elite paratroop battalion. Then I made a State visit to France, where I was welcomed with all the etiquette one could wish for on such an occasion – a Republican Guard escort on horseback, a State banquet and so on – and that, I should stress, at a time when Africa, and so the Congo, was very critical of France's policy in relation to Chad, especially the strong military presence it maintained there. When I was President of the OAU, there was also a period of great tension between France and Libya at the time when the Prime Minister, Jacques Chirac, was a political opponent of President Mitterrand. The French President met Colonel Gadaffi in Crete. The meeting was unproductive and the question was whether France should continue talks with Libya. Chirac was in favour, Mitterrand against. In fact, there was no follow-up to the meeting.

– *How did you react at the France-Africa summit at La Baule in June 1990 when François Mitterrand told African governments they would have to make their countries more democratic if they were to continue to receive aid ? At the time, several African Heads of State were very irritated by his speech, which some saw as interventionism or at least inappropriate lecturing.*

I felt what he said was pointless and certainly insensitive. I didn't personally respond because I didn't feel his words were aimed at me. There was a good reason for this : at the time of the La Baule summit, discussions were underway in the Congo about the necessary democratisation of our country, the prelude to our National Conference. More specifically, we were discussing the best way of introducing a multiparty system.

In any case, that sort of blackmail was pointless since, as we subsequently saw, this aid for so-called "democratised" countries never materialised ! Worse, it was a very rash and even dangerous way of launching democratisation processes in some African countries that weren't necessarily prepared for it. We saw the results with these National Conferences, which were more insurrectional arenas than true democratic forums. They seriously destabilised a number of French-speaking African States, although things did go relatively smoothly in some countries, especially Benin — but not, I think, without some French involvement at one level or another. I have no wish to deny the merits of the Beninese people's National Conference, but, well...

— *So why did this only happen in French-speaking countries ?*

Exactly because of that kind of compulsion. No such pressure was applied to English-speaking countries, for instance, which continued to be governed by single-party regimes for a very long time. The French-speaking States were treated in a cavalier fashion! I think the method was clearly wrong in these cases. In fact, I should point out that at the same summit at La Baule, another, equally important speech challenged François Mitterrand's declaration: the speech made by Hassan II.

— *What did the King of Morocco say ?*

He was rather irritated by François Mitterrand's speech. In fact, that's an understatement! Basically, he reminded him that it was up to the peoples themselves to decide on their future, no-one could introduce democracy in their place! That was an extremely clear answer!

— *Did the La Baule summit change anything in your relations with the French President ?*

It didn't affect them at all.

— *After François Mitterrand came Jacques Chirac, said to be your friend.*

I think that the value of the friendly personal relationship I had with President Chirac lay in our mutual respect. We met during the Cold War, in the days when the single party – the Congolese

Party of Labour – was in power at home, and our government was very much to the left, while as you know, Jacques Chirac is a right-winger. Well, that was never a problem : we respected each other's convictions. I'd go even further : it didn't prevent us from enjoying a friendly relationship. At no point were the affairs of our respective States affected in any way. We obviously put the interest of our States before our own personal interests. I'd known Jacques Chirac when he was Mayor of Paris. He played a major role in the International Association of French-Speaking Mayors and, as a Gaullist, he had great respect for Brazzaville, the capital of Free France. In fact, when we celebrated the first centenary of our capital, as Mayor of Paris, Jacques Chirac came at the head of a large delegation to attend the events we'd organised. Indeed, it was Jacques Chirac who had the superb French Cultural Centre built in Brazzaville. We owe it to his attachment to Brazzaville and the Congo, and not – as some may have imagined – to "Françafrique"[1] !

– *We'll come back to "Françafrique" in a moment. First, if you don't mind, perhaps we can finish this portrait gallery of French presidents with Nicolas Sarkozy, a pre-*

---

1. Here, "Françafrique" refers to a special relationship between France and its former African colonies, involving shadowy financial and political links.

sident you've received in the Congo[1]. Did you already know him ?

Yes, I knew him before he was President of the Republic, when he was Minister of the Budget and then Minister of the Interior. Today, we have a friendly and even warm relationship, which has further developed since his official visit to Brazzaville. That led to a significant rapprochement between our two countries. I can safely say we're in total harmony.

— When you heard Nicolas Sarkozy declare in Dakar in July 2007 that "the tragedy of Africa is that the African has never entered history enough", how did you react ?

Well, I think that if the African had never entered history, the Egyptian pyramids would never have existed. Even the Arabs who are in Egypt today weren't there at the time. And if the African hadn't entered history, we wouldn't have discovered the very distant ancestors of humanity in today's Chad, as well as in the east of our continent. All scientists now agree that the cradle of humanity was in Africa. In short, I think it's better to move on. Nobody in France defends that kind of argument any more. In fact, when he visited Brazzaville, President Sarkozy addressed our Par-

---

1. In March 2009.

liament gathered in Congress, and his speech was much appreciated, just like the one made in Cape Town. Both set the record straight.

— In his speech in Dakar, Nicolas Sarkozy called slavery a crime against Africans, a crime against humans and a crime against humanity. He added: "No-one can ask today's generations to atone for this crime committed by past generations. No-one can ask sons to show remorse for the misdeeds of their fathers." What do you think about remorse?

That's an easy question for me to answer because I've already made a declaration on the subject before the Assembly General of the United Nations in New York. That was in 2000. I said then that the time had come for the UN to rule that the slave trade was a "crime against humanity". Naturally, this wasn't so that Africa might demand any compensation or damages. No, at the start of a new millennium, I simply hoped we could sum up that sinister page of history and be able to move on.

— More generally, do you think remorse is necessary?

It costs nothing to recognise that at one point in history, a group of men did something unpardonable. I feel it's right that in all humility, we should recognise the deplorable things that have happened in the history of humanity, over the centuries as in the last century, whether these are Nazism, Fascism or Rwanda. After that, we can move on.

— *In fact, the question of remorse isn't an issue in relation to the slave trade, the holocaust or the genocide in Rwanda. I was going to say remorse is obvious in such cases. The issue is other events in history that weren't necessarily totally negative, where even the very principle of remorse is debatable. It's true that all States have been built on violence and some say that if we begin to express remorse for all the violence done in the history of humanity and focus too much on the past, we risk fanning fires that haven't been properly extinguished, or being unable to move on. What do you think ?*

What do you expect to happen ? Look at Italy. Now reconciliation's a reality, no-one's going to try and challenge Italian unity. Who'll argue with the 1885 Treaty of Berlin, the prelude to the "carving up" of Africa, when it was chopped into pieces to suit interests that weren't those of its populations ? Nobody's going to contest today's frontiers on our continent. After all, when they founded the OAU, the Africans themselves recognised their States within their colonial borders. Even so, it doesn't mean that Africa being divided up to suit the interests of others was a good thing !

– 15 –

"FRANÇAFRIQUE" ?

An unknown concept – The France-Africa Summits – Emigration and the "brain drain"

– Earlier, we mentioned "Françafrique". It undeniably existed.

If it existed, then we in the Congo were unaware of its shape and colour. It may have existed. If some people were involved, it's up to you to find them and talk to them about it. In any case, here, we never knew what "Françafrique" was ! If it was a new form of colonialism, that's something we've always firmly opposed in the Congo. We've never hosted military bases or concluded any secret defence agreements with France. Could President Fulbert have entered into such agreements when the Congo won independence ? If he did, we found no evidence of it in 1963, when he was toppled by the revolution. So we can say that from the Sixties up to the present day, the only co-

131

operation agreements we've entered into with France are those that benefit both parties.

– In any case, we can say there are special relationships between France and the French-speaking countries of Africa, without necessarily employing the term "Françafrique", which does have slightly neo-colonialist overtones.

If there are special relationships, they can only be expressed in State agreements. The Congo has no agreements with France that might suggest that certain State business may be conducted covertly, through some shadowy agency or lobby. We've never had situations of that kind here !

– Do you think the France-Africa summits still serve a purpose today ? Are they actually useful and efficient ?

I think they're necessary and useful. They give us all a chance to meet and discuss our methods of co-operation and the best ways to assist development. Every two years, similar summits bring together the countries of Africa and Japan. We've had three meetings of that kind. The last was in Yokohama in 2008. Then we have the same type of summit with India and China. We also have regular ministerial conferences of all Africa with the United States of America. So why not with France ? If that's an expression of "Françafrique" – "Franceafrica" – then what about "Japanafrica",

"Indafrica", "Chinafrica", "Americafrica" and so on ?

– Turning to the question of Congolese emigration to France, apparently there aren't very many migrants.

No, the Congolese aren't the largest immigrant population in France. We've signed migration agreements with the French government, but they're based on a principle of co-operation over migration rather than selected migration. We've changed the concept. Previously, France chose the immigrants it allowed in. Today, there are agreements that determine the conditions in which populations can move from one country to another. We can't talk about globalisation and then refuse the movement of persons !

– Although one of the issues raised by a certain type of African emigration – I'm thinking of the emigration of students – is that all too often, they don't return to their native country at the end of their studies, but prefer to remain in Europe or America, where they're better paid.

That's the "brain drain". The most serious problem, though, is that these managers and professionals are trained at the expense of African States, but then work for countries that haven't contributed to their training. That's a genuine issue. In fact, it should be a question of conscience for them. Many say they don't have decent working conditions or modern equipment and material in Africa, which is true. It's also true that they're better paid in Europe. But if all Africans reasoned in that way, there would never have been any managerial or professional classes in Africa, they'd all have stayed in London or Paris ! It's up to the Congolese, up to us, to overcome these difficulties and create a better situation in the country, if not for this generation, then at least for the next. There's room for discussion, but it's true that we can't continue to train professional classes who don't reciprocate by using what they learn for the benefit of their fellow citizens who have contributed to their training abroad with their taxes.

— *As has been suggested in some countries, are you considering asking your students who have gone abroad and who settle there after their studies to repay the cost of their education covered by the Congolese State ?*

There are no plans for such a policy here as yet. I don't know if such a measure has been applied anywhere else or if it's proved effective if it has been. I think it's better that we should maintain an honest dialogue with these professional classes, continue to talk to them. Since it's our duty, we must also continue to improve working conditions here and also improve salaries — why not ? I think that if we enter into discussions on this question with Congolese graduates abroad, it could produce results.

— Does the Congo have a special relationship with Euro-pean countries other than France ?

We have relations with the European Union as a whole. Also, we obviously have bilateral relations for specific projects or programmes. Italy's ENI, for instance, is one of the companies extracting our oil. Then there are Portuguese companies established in the Congo. One of them, ESCOM, is building an airport at Ollombo, 400 kilometres to the north of Brazzaville, funded by the Congolese government. A Portuguese bank is also planning to come and do business in the Congo.

16

AFRICAN PORTRAITS

"The Old Man" – Samora Machel – Sankara's fatigues – An evening with Hassan II – The OAU and the Western Sahara

– A person's merit is inherent, of course, but it's also related to those things they admire, which can help define them better. Among the African Heads of State you've met, which ones have made a strong impression on you, President?

I'd start with Félix Houphouët-Boigny or the "Old Man" as he was affectionately known. He was a very wise man who was remarkably successful at combining African tradition – especially a way of managing people that's specific to our continent – and a modern style to ensure his country's progress in the world. He wasn't only wise, but skilful too.

– Have other personalities left their mark on you in one way or another?

I was close to Samora Machel who led the liberation struggle in Mozambique and who was a man of strong convictions. He believed in our struggle, like Marien Ngouabi and Thomas Sankara. The President of Burkina Faso had an ideal and believed in it. We were close and I spent long hours talking with him.

— *He was a little provocative.*

I don't know. Call it that if you want. His attitude may sometimes have been dictated by the brutality of the time... his particular way of saying out loud what others were thinking to themselves. Yes, that could be seen as provocation, but I'm not sure it was.

— *Even when he attended international diplomatic conferences in fatigues with a revolver at his waist ?*

That wasn't provocation ! Fidel Castro has spent his whole life like that, without offending anyone. I used to wear military dress myself for many years. It was Sankara's style ! But I can assure you he was a courteous, intelligent lad.

— *In quite another vein, I know that you greatly admire Hassan II. You met him two days before his death, I believe.*

It was in July 1999. The King of Morocco had invited President Bongo and me to dinner in his palace in Skhirat. The dinner went on very late into the night. We talked, talked a great deal, but we mainly listened to the King.

— *What subjects did you discuss?*

We talked about the international situation and especially Africa. I can't tell you more than that. What I can tell you, though, is that the King showed a very detailed knowledge of the workings of our world and impressive analytical skills. For us, it was rewarding as well as a very great pleasure to listen to him. That night – and it was the first time I saw him do that at the table – Hassan II took his medication in public. At one point in the meal, they brought him quite a few tablets and he took them in front of us. That was a very unusual thing for him to do. President Bongo and I saw it as a mark of trust as he prepared to leave this world. We were deeply touched.

— *At that dinner, did Hassan II mention his succession?*

Not exactly. He spoke of his country and the Western Sahara question. With a slight lump in his throat, he told us he would have liked to settle that problem himself, because he didn't want to leave such a legacy to his son. We remained with him until after midnight. Three days later, I was in Oyo when I learned of his death. I flew to Rabat immediately.

– Hassan II was Arab, but also African. Did you ever talk to him – not necessarily on that evening – about his relations with sub-Saharan Africa ?

Yes, even on that evening. I'll give you an actual example. At that dinner, he told Bongo and me, "It's not enough to talk about co-operation with the Gulf States, you have to act too !" He then made a suggestion : "You have forests in Gabon and in the Congo. Find a logging permit in Gabon and a logging permit in the Congo. Organise the non-consumptive use of those forests. Let's produce wood. We'll help you export the production to the Gulf States. They need wood and they don't have any." I thought that was a very shrewd proposal, a good example of a potential triangular relationship between sub-Saharan Africa, North Africa and the Gulf States. Unfortunately, the project fell through after the death of the King.

– Didn't you also meet Hassan II at the height of the OAU crisis when you were President of the Organisation in 1986 to 1987, a crisis resulting from the Western Sahara issue, in fact ?

I must say his attitude impressed me greatly at the time. Morocco had just left the OAU because

of the Western Sahara question. Like many African
States, the Congo recognised the Sahrawi Arab
Democratic Republic proclaimed by the Polisario
Front, which was fighting for the territory's independence. The OAU was genuinely on the verge
of implosion because of this issue : the divisions
between those in favour of independence and
those against it were too great for there to be any
chance of settling them. It must be remembered
that this was certainly one of the most serious
crises the organisation ever faced ! So when I asked
to meet His Majesty Hassan II to discuss the problem, I didn't expect him to accept, far from it !
Yet he immediately agreed to receive me in Fez. I
was surprised and even struck by his decision : he
could just as well have refused, given the circumstances and especially my country's recognition of
the SADR. I had a serious discussion with him and
we examined the issue in depth. We agreed that
the problem was explosive, the cause of major divisions in Africa and even potentially fatal for the
OAU, so too dangerous to leave in the hands of
the organisation. Consequently, it was during my
term as President of the OAU and in association
with the King of Morocco that we were able to
pass on the Western Sahara question to the United
Nations, which is still responsible for it today.

— *But in saving African unity, you deferred the handling*
— *and so the solution* — *of the Western Sahara question,*

since the United Nations have been unable to find an answer.

We didn't intend to defer the question, we mainly wanted to find the most appropriate and least dangerous context in which it could be examined. We also felt that the United Nations had greater freedom of action and more material resources than the OAU. After all, the United Nations are there to tackle questions that can no longer be managed on a regional level. It's normal practice for a region to pass on a problem on which it can't make any further progress to the United Nations. The differences of opinion were too great within the OAU ; we'd reached a stalemate.

17

AT SOUTHERN AFRICA'S SIDE

The Africa Fund – A meeting with
the "Iron Lady" – Celebrations over
the Atlantic

*– Last but not least, we should end this portrait gallery
of the great Africans you admire with a word on Nelson
Mandela, a man who's very close to you. We'll come to him
in a moment, but first, to understand the relationship of
very strong mutual respect that unites you, we should remind
ourselves that the Congo was seen as one of the most active
countries in the struggle for the liberation of Southern
Africa.*

The Congo supported all liberation struggles in
Africa. In the Angolan conflict, we gave direct and
very active support to the MPLA. In fact, the organisation was based in Brazzaville for nearly fifteen
years. We also provided effective aid to the
SWAPO in Namibia and it broadcast its radio programmes from our capital. We stood side by side
with all the other liberation movements throug-

hout the continent, whether in Mozambique, Guinea-Bissau or Zimbabwe, working directly with them or through the Liberation Committee of the OAU. So, the struggle against apartheid in South Africa was naturally a priority for us, a symbolic battle to be waged constantly.

— In fact, the liberation of Southern Africa was the main issue of your first term of office at the head of the Organisation of African Unity from 1986-1987 [1].

It was for that reason that I asked the Non-Aligned Movement summit in Harare, Zimbabwe, to make a tangible commitment to the struggle to end apartheid. I suggested that a fund which I called the "Africa Fund" should be set up for that purpose and all the Non-Aligned nations asked to contribute. I received immediate support from India's Rajiv Gandhi, Cuba's Fidel Castro and Robert Mugabe, who was hosting the conference. The Fund was set up and all the member countries of the Non-Aligned Movement made financial or material contributions to the front-line nations. In the same spirit, as President of the Congo and President of the OAU, I organised a world symposium in Brazzaville for writers against apartheid, based on the theme : "Writers accuse apartheid" [2].

1. See appendix II.
2. See appendix III.

This symposium, attended by writers from all over Africa and the rest of the world, had a great impact, far beyond purely intellectual circles.

These initiatives among others helped speed up the liberation process in Southern Africa. The time had finally come. All the largest nations, including the United States – which had long resisted the idea – had finally agreed on the principle of economic sanctions against South Africa.

It seems self-evident today, but at the time, I can assure you it wasn't. I'll give you an example. As President of the OAU, I was campaigning to ensure that as many countries as possible would impose sanctions on the Pretoria regime. In one year, I toured the great capitals : Washington, Moscow, Paris, Beijing, Bonn, Ottawa, Brussels, Stockholm, Oslo and others. Then I obviously visited London, where I was received by the Prime Minister of the time, Mrs. Thatcher, who welcomed me very politely over a cup of coffee. After explaining the reasons for my initiative, I asked her if she would agree to offer her support by imposing economic sanctions on South Africa. She listened to my arguments carefully, then, looking me straight in the eye, she said : "President, why do you want to destroy an economy that works ?" So you see, it wasn't a foregone conclusion.

– *What did you reply ?*

I answered, "Prime Minister, that country's economy may work, but at what a price !"

— *Returning to the "Africa Fund", the Congo was particularly generous.*

In any case, the whole country swung into action, from the oldest to the youngest and the richest to the poorest, and from local shops to the government. We launched a great national movement, asking every inhabitant of the Congo, whoever they were and whatever their age, to give something, even just a few CFA francs[1] if that were all they could manage. We even urged schoolchildren to ask their parents for a coin or banknote to give to their teacher who was responsible for collecting money for the Fund. This mobilisation of our country's entire population to support that great cause was a complete success.

— *How did you learn of Nelson Mandela's release ?*

If you don't mind, before we talk about the great, historic moment of Mandela's release, I'd like to look back briefly over the months that led up to it. It was at that time that we hosted a conference bringing together Angola, South Africa and Cuba

---

1. African Financial Community francs, a currency used in French-speaking countries in Africa.

in Brazzaville. With the United States acting as a mediator, the aim was to find a solution for the Angolan conflict, which had reached a stalemate. All diplomatic attempts to resolve the impasse had been a total failure. Meanwhile, there was no visible progress towards imminent independence in Namibia. The United States' position was that all Cuban troops should leave Angola without delay and they linked that issue to Namibian independence. As long as a single Cuban soldier remained in Angola, the UN resolution for the liberation of Namibia couldn't be implemented. At least the deal was clear. The negotiations were very closely-argued and complex. They continued for several months, finally resulting in what was called the "Brazzaville Protocol", signed on the 22nd December 1988. The Protocol was adopted at the UN and led Namibia towards independence.

This development was to herald changes in policy on the part of the South-African regime, as well as different democratisation processes that began in Southern Africa and, finally, the freeing of Nelson Mandela. So what happened in Brazzaville was a crucial turning point in the liberation of a large part of Africa. Like all the Congolese, I'm proud of our country's role. Following the agreement and to pay tribute to the part the Congo had played, President Bush officially invited me to pay a state visit to the United States. As I was flying over the Atlantic to Washington, the pilot announced that Nelson Mandela had just been freed !

– I doubt if there'd ever been such celebrations on a plane !

Indeed, it was indescribable ! All the Congolese on the plane were jumping for joy, laughing, crying, shouting and bouncing in their seats. In fact, there was so much movement that I asked the pilot if there was any risk of it interfering with the balance of the plane. He reassured me, of course : "As long as they don't leave their seats, the passengers can make all the noise they like and drink as much as they want !" And they did, I can assure you ! There wasn't a bottle of champagne on the plane that wasn't emptied ! So it was in a plane above the Atlantic, on my way to America, that I gave my first statement expressing my joy at the release of Nelson Mandela.

– When did you meet Nelson Mandela for the first time ?

At the proclamation of Namibian independence in Windhoek. Later, he came on an official visit to Brazzaville to address the Congolese people and thank them for their efforts in support of the liberation of Southern Africa.

On this occasion – it was in February 1991 – I talked to Nelson Mandela at length. We discussed

Africa of course, and Southern Africa in particular. I was impressed by his concern for the problems of his people. He especially spoke of his great concern for the difficulties that South-African exiles returning to their country with no means or resources might face. I assured him of our complete solidarity and offered our support. That evening, at a banquet at the Presidential Residence – it was nearly midnight – Nelson began to dance to the music ! Myriam Makeba was there. Suddenly overcome with emotion, she burst into tears. Turning to me, she said : "That's the first time he's danced since he was freed !"

– *Who is Nelson Mandela, the man, for you ?*

For Africans, Nelson Mandela is the symbol, the embodiment, of freedom. I should add that he symbolises tolerance too. His courage is equalled only by his love of humanity, especially the suffering and humiliated, of course. Have you looked closely at Nelson Mandela's smile ? You must have noticed that he smiles a lot. Don't you think that, apart from his happiness at finally living in freedom in a free country, it also expresses the pleasure he takes in talking to others, and the interest and respect he feels for them ? Behind that smile, there's also the fierce determination that enabled him to hold out for nearly thirty years in his country's jails without weakening even once, without giving up his fight for human dignity and freedom for a second. People like him are rare, too rare in our world, so to enjoy the privilege of his friendship is a genuine honour!

HEARING THE VOICE OF AFRICA

Crises : DRC, Darfur,
Ivory Coast, Zimbabwe

— This may not be an easy question to answer, President, but have you ever contacted a Head of State with whom you have a close relationship when you feel they're in difficulty for one reason or another ?

It's out of the question to interfere in the affairs of another State, but we can make contact when there's a crisis. It all depends on the personal relations we have with a particular leader. If relations are good, we can always share our opinion on a specific issue. For instance, when I was President of the African Union in 2006, there was a presidential election in the Democratic Republic of the Congo. Given the rather inflexible positions of the different parties, I thought it might be useful for the candidates to meet for a day or two in the presence of chosen personalities and agree on a code of conduct before the campaign began. President Kabila and Vice-President Bemba were both candidates and relations between them were very strained at the time. I suggested this meeting, which would be attended by the President of Gabon among others. It was to be held in Oyo in the Congo. President Kabila agreed in principle.

— And so ?

Well, it wasn't possible to hold the meeting. You'll forgive me if I don't explain why. However, it was suggested. So to answer your question, I think it's acceptable to give advice. It can be followed or not. The main thing is to encourage dialogue at all times.

— Can the AU really make its voice heard in Africa ? When we see crisis after crisis — Ivory Coast, the DRC, Kenya, Darfur, et cetera — we get the feeling that the Union isn't properly equipped to solve the problems that Africa faces.

The means to intervene may be lacking, but that doesn't mean there's no desire to intervene. I think we have to distinguish between the two things. On the questions of Darfur, Ivory Coast, Kenya and even Zimbabwe, the African Union has always intervened — firmly, even. In the case of Darfur, the African Union was the first organisation to send in troops. Seven thousand men were deployed there. It was the first time Africa had done such a thing and it was done ! I was President of the African Union during part of those operations. We may have been short of logistical support and forced to call on other powers for assistance, but we did intervene. During the Ivory Coast crisis too, we made every effort to resolve the differences between the parties.

— *The differences between the parties were resolved at the Marcoussis conference in France.*

They were resolved at Marcoussis, yes, but not without the African Union deciding to intervene. Yet even after Marcoussis, the Ivory Coast crisis continued to worsen ! I was President of the African Union at the time, so I can explain in detail. The AU played a major role on the Committee for Peace and Security, which met a number of times to examine the Ivory Coast and Darfur issues, especially when agreement was needed for United Nations forces to enter Darfur. That wasn't easy to obtain, since some African countries – especially Arab ones – were strongly opposed. Finally, we had to make great efforts to enable today's situation : a large number of peacekeeping troops deployed under the joint command of the United Nations and the African Union.

— *Looking at Zimbabwe, do you think that more coercive measures should have been aimed at Robert Mugabe's regime ?*

That's partly what happened. Africa handed the problem over to the international sub-region, which is now dealing with it. It may have taken a long time, but the compromise on a government of union that was recently achieved[1] was enabled by Africa and Africa alone.

– Do you think it's enough ?

Do you think it's necessary to go further than a political compromise that's been accepted by the people of Zimbabwe and the international community ?

---

1. In January 2009.

THE UNITED STATES OF AFRICA ?

One Africa or 53 ? – Pan-Africanism – Vulnerable regional groupings – Religions and democracy

– There's the feeling that Africa still finds it hard to intervene on a certain number of burning issues and so appears fragile. It's hard to achieve unity and it's very often difficult to reconcile different points of view. Is there truly an Africa or are there really fifty-three ?

We Africans are determined to work together to achieve development. I'm with those who believe that since the world is organised into major political and economic groupings today, Africa must do the same. Yet between the intention and the act, between the goal to be achieved and the method... I think that in today's Africa, we disagree more on the method.

– More precisely ?

I think there are those who believe we should
be taking immediate steps towards union — by forming a government, for instance — and those who
think that more method is needed, that history
hasn't yet shown it's possible to achieve this kind
of result in an authoritarian way. Look at the European Union. It wasn't built in a day and even now,
it's moving forward in small steps.

*— But isn't it a matter of urgency ? We're facing a crisis
and Africa's in a position of weakness to deal with it.
Wouldn't it be best to accelerate the process of union to help
Africa defend itself ?*

The crisis should help speed up the process of
union, but I think that to be credible here — and
we need to be credible ! — we must do more than
just make declarations. It's vital we win over our
partners. If we were serious about union, we would
have speeded up the sub-regional integration process, for instance. Yet when I look at the progress
these groups — the regional economic communities — have made, the results are quite disappoin-
ting. The Arab Maghreb Union[1] is at a complete
standstill for various reasons. The ECOWAS[2] has
made some progress, but we can't really say it's
shown any great desire for integration. The same

1. Founded in 1989, the AMU has five Member States.
2. The Economic Community of West African States,
founded in 1975, has fifteen Member States.

is true of the Economic Community of Central African States[1]. Although the SADC[2] has benefited from the positive legacy of jointly-waged liberation struggles, it is destabilised by South Africa's influence compared to that of its other members and its results are still limited. The East African Community[3] is in its early days and hasn't yet proved itself. So I side with those who think that to be convincing, we must first take firmer steps in our regional economic committees, making them more active and vigorous. When that's been achieved, the process of integration on a higher level may well speed up of itself, driven by a genuine political will to make progress. If ten or so countries apply their capacity for integration, that may be enough to move the continent forward. Let's take the example of the European Union again. It started out with six countries, but there are twenty-seven today, with others knocking on the door.

— That means Nkrumah's pan-Africanism[4] will have to wait !

---

1. Founded in 1983, the ECCAS has ten Member States.
2. The Southern African Development Community, formed in 1992, includes fourteen countries.
3. Reformed in 2001, the EAC has five Member States.
4. Kwame Nkrumah (1909-1972) was the first President of the Republic of Ghana from 1957 to 1966, one of the founding fathers of the OAU in 1963 and a convinced supporter and champion of pan-Africanism.

Nkrumah's ambition has to be seen in the perspective of his day. Africa was just freeing itself of colonisation. The Non-Aligned Movement was a genuine force between the communist East and capitalist West, and many hopes were invested in it. Don't forget that on the one side, there were the strategic interests of the great powers, and on the other, the newly-independent States' search for means of survival, which led them to come out in favour of one bloc or the other. That was the situation in the days of Nkrumah. It's different today.

— So you're even less inclined to share the idea put forward by the President of Senegal, Abdoulaye Wade, who says that it's in Africa's interest to unite, not only to deal with the crisis, but also to avoid being "overtaken" by emergent nations — China, India and Brazil. He believes that the continent should rapidly select a joint Minister of Foreign Affairs or even a President, and even suggests a possible future capital of Africa : Sikasso, in Mali !

Can we make something happen just by announcing it ? How can we talk about a united Africa when Senegal and The Gambia can't even manage to form a confederation ? You only have to look at a map ! The Gambia's like a tongue in the mouth of Senegal, so an alliance between the two countries, or even something more, seems very obvious from every point of view. Let me ask what convinced pan-Africanist is not at least in favour of a confederation of Senegal and The Gambia? Well, I'd add that if this pan-Africanist is unable to achieve such a goal, and, moving up a level, they're unable to achieve the political union of West Africa, based on the ECOWAS, for example, how do they imagine they'll be able to achieve the unity of all Africa on a still higher level : an entire continent? That seems unrealistic to me. Perhaps I'm wrong, but I think that if we're to be effective, we have to take things as they are in reality and move them forward. We should avoid rushing headlong into anything, because we don't know where it might lead us.

We Africans have a habit. Every ten years we organise an initiative on this issue. In 1980, it was the Lagos Plan of Action, which launched the regional communities, but was never properly implemented. In 1991, it was the Abuja Treaty, a pioneering examination of ways and means to work towards an African government. That wasn't properly implemented either. Then in 2001, we decided to move towards economic and social integration with the adoption of the NEPAD [1], none of whose declared aims has been achieved to date.

— Still on this issue of pan-Africanism, some speak rather simplistically of an Arab, Muslim "white Africa", and an Animist, Christian "black Africa" — although this

---

1. New Partnership for Africa's Development.

perceived division is being superseded with the rise of Islam to the south of the Sahara. Don't you think religion may slow African integration? After all, each religion has its customs, its rules, even its laws.

I don't think so. If there should be the political will to achieve African integration one day, I believe it will include both the North and South. Africa is one and its populations sense this. In any case, as you said, Islam is established to the south of the Sahara and even if the Christian religions aren't predominant in the north of the continent, they still exist. I don't think these religious rifts can divide Africa.

— Not even the Islamists?

Fundamentalists aren't accepted in Africa, either in the north or south.

— But there's strong pressure...

Pressure?

— Al-Qaeda Maghreb is active.

Al-Qaeda is opposed in Tunisia, Algeria, Morocco, Mauritania and Sudan too. I can assure you that the fundamentalists aren't accepted anywhere in Africa, either in the north or the south!

Africa's leaders and peoples are very vigilant on this issue.

– What role do you think religion should play in a democracy ?

First and foremost, there must be respect for basic freedoms. As long as the principles are clear, the citizen's freedom of choice of religion is a personal matter. It isn't the State's business. The separation of religion and the State must be clear : what is God's is God's and what is Caesar's is Caesar's. If this principle is applied, no problems are possible ! I can't see why religions shouldn't contribute to the education or spiritual training of populations in accordance with the wishes of different groups. Once again, that's a personal matter. As long as everyone's individual freedoms, for which the State is responsible, are secure.

– Aren't there any religious problems in the Congo ?

No, the Congolese are free to choose their religion and practise it as they wish. In fact, the first President of the Congo, Father Fulbert Youlou, was a Catholic priest, and the elected President of the Transitional Parliament during the National Conference was Bishop Ernest Kombo.

– You yourself are a freemason ?

DENIS SASSOU NGUESSO

Like many men and women throughout the world, from Mozart to Abraham Lincoln. That's entirely a matter for me. Would you ask me that question if I were European ?

– 20 –

A SEAT FOR AFRICA
Three hypotheses

– Although some are in favour of it, Africa still doesn't have a permanent seat on the United Nations Security Council. Do you think it will succeed in making its voice heard there one day ?

People with privileges are never in a hurry to give them up ! Even so, it's obvious that we'll be represented there sooner or later – sooner would be better, of course. But apart from the issue of a permanent seat for Africa on the United Nations Security Council, I think the United Nations is in need of reform. After all, it was founded just after the Second World War and that was a long time ago ! Since then, the world has changed and is still changing rapidly. You must agree that relationships between States today aren't the same as they were in 1945 ! I'd be very surprised if those who are resisting these changes can hold out for long.

163

— If the UN gave Africa a permanent seat on the Security Council, what country might take it ?

Don't worry, we'll deal with that ! In fact, several proposals have been circulating in Africa and are already being discussed.

— What are they ?

The first is that any representative of Africa should be chosen by the African Union. The second proposal is that because of their demographic or economic weight, certain countries think they should naturally be candidates – these include South Africa, Nigeria and Egypt, and perhaps others too. The third proposal is for a rotation on a regional basis, a method already applied to the presidency of the African Union : first a representative of North Africa, then a representative of sub-Saharan Africa, and so on, with a periodicity to be determined. As you can see, we have plenty of inspiration !

— What would you prefer ?

I don't want to say for the moment. The debate is underway and we shouldn't count our chickens before they're hatched. First, it must be recognised that Africa has the right to a permanent seat on the United Nations Security Council, then we'll get together and examine how we should be represented. In fact, I should point out that we're not asking for one, but *two* seats ! Once again, though, I think our priority should be to examine overall reform of the United Nations system, if only to give more weight to the decisions of the General Assembly.

— Can you count on the support of France over the need for a permanent African seat on the UN Security Council ?

Apparently. But that aside, if tomorrow you asked a Chilean, an Italian, an Australian, a Vietnamese or any other inhabitant of this planet who isn't African, "Do you think that Africa should sit as a permanent member on the UN Security Council ?", what do you think they'd answer ? Do you believe they'd think it right that a continent representing fifty-three countries shouldn't have a seat at the table where the future of the world is discussed, when all the other continents have a seat there ? In fact, it would be well worth holding a global referendum on the issue. Why not ? In any case, I'm suggesting the idea !

A REGION IN THE MAKING

The Gulf of Guinea Commission
– Relations with Presidents Bongo
and Dos Santos

— Earlier, you said that the priority should be to accomplish the realisation of African unity in stages, and that these stages would initially involve the construction of solid regional organisations. I imagine it was in this spirit that you anticipated the creation of the Gulf of Guinea Commission, which has been joined by the countries of the Atlantic Coast of Africa from Nigeria to Angola today ?

I suggested the idea to Presidents Obasanjo of Nigeria and Bongo of Gabon in 1999. I saw the Gulf of Guinea as a strategic region and thought that the neighbouring countries should join forces in a community of dialogue and interest. There was no shortage of subjects for discussion : shipping, fishing, trade, port infrastructure, offshore oil, security and pollution, not to mention strategic and territorial issues. Our commission examines many questions and functions perfectly. Its headquarters are in Luanda and its current Secretary-General is the former President of São Tomé and Príncipe, Miguel Trovoada.

— Can you give us a concrete example of a case handled by the Commission ?

Not long ago, this kind of dialogue-based body showed its worth when it settled a territorial dispute between Cameroon and Nigeria over the Bakassi peninsula. Today, the case of Mbanié Island between Gabon and Equatorial Guinea is on the Commission's agenda.

— You have both political and family ties with President Bongo. Your eldest daughter, Édith Lucie, was his wife until her death in March 2009. How do you get on with him ?

Take a look at a map of Africa and see where Gabon is located. To the north, it shares part of its frontier with Equatorial Guinea and part with Cameroon, while all the rest of its territory has a long frontier shared with the Congo. I don't need to tell you that you find the same populations, the same ethnic groups and the same families on either side of the border. Here and throughout Africa, we inherited the frontiers decided by the European colonial powers in the 1885 Treaty of Berlin. The reality is that families were "sliced" in two ! It explains how close we are to Gabon. There was even a time in the colonial period when the two countries formed a single territory called Middle Congo.

— President Bongo and you are two Heads of State with two strong personalities. I believe there have been times of great friendship between you, as well as rather more delicate and even difficult episodes.

Essentially, our relations have been good and remain so, even in the political domain. It's good that we can talk directly and even frankly at times, and we feel free to do so. It's true that our relations were somewhat strained at one point with the rise of Lissouba in Congolese politics. For ethnic reasons, Lissouba was close to President Bongo, who found himself in an extremely awkward position because of this. It grew even more awkward when the situation became very tense here, with a man he saw as family for ethnic reasons on one side, and a man he saw as a blood relation on the other ! He was in a very conflictual situation and I understand why he sometimes found himself in difficulty...

— What about today ?

Today, there are no problems of any kind.

– You also go back a long way with another president of a neighbouring country : President Eduardo Dos Santos of Angola.

Compared to my relationship with President Bongo, my relations with President Dos Santos are more political and even ideological. I knew him for fifteen years in Brazzaville, where the MPLA had its rear base. He was one of the young officials under Agostinho Neto, who became the first President of independent Angola. When I was Minister of Defence from 1975 to 1976, at the height of the war that brought the MPLA to power in Luanda, I saw him even more often. We provided the MPLA with help when FNLA troops were just fifteen kilometres from Luanda, encircling the city and preparing to take it. That was the great battle of Nandongo, fifteen kilometres from Luanda, the decisive struggle won by Neto's men. At the time, I was the Congo's Minister of Defence and in direct, virtually permanent contact with my opposite number in the MPLA, Iko Carreira. So you can imagine how closely I was involved in these events !

– On the subject of Angola, are there still discussions about the future of Cabinda, the Angolan province enclosed between two French-speaking countries, the Congo and the DRC, or is the question settled ?

It's actually an enclave colonised by the Portuguese, hemmed in between two French-speaking countries as a result of the absurd division of Africa decided by the European colonisers in Berlin in 1885. At the time, African territories were carved up like joints of meat ! Look at my country, for instance. When you follow the border between the Congo and the DRC along the Congo river, it would be completely feasible to follow the river down to the sea and take that as the border, but the colonisers decided otherwise. As soon as you pass Brazzaville, a few kilometres to the south of our capital, the border no longer follows the river, but cuts across land. I don't know what kind of bargaining led to this agreement between the French and Belgians. The result is very strange, not to mention the fact that it artificially separated ethnic groups and families. It was the same principle that led to the creation of the province of Cabinda, a Portuguese-speaking enclave between two French-speaking countries, the Congo and the DRC. To answer your question, there's no problem over the Cabinda enclave. It's in everyone's interest to ensure lasting stability in this region of Africa.

— Doesn't that contradict what you said about a possible Senegal-The Gambia confederation ? Shouldn't Cabinda become part of the international sub-region in one way or another ?

But it's already part of the ECCAS ! Anyway, I don't think we can draw a parallel with Senegal and The Gambia. Cabinda is a province of Angola, not a country. Also, it's not within another country, but located between the Congo and the DRC.

– 22 –

ON THE OTHER SIDE OF THE OCEAN

9/11 – History in the making –
The risks of the Internet
– Obama brings hope

– How did the events of the 11ᵗʰ September 2001 affect you ?

On that day, I was working in my office with one of my staff when my eldest daughter, Édith Lucie, called me from Paris to tell me to turn on a television news channel. I did so immediately, just as the second plane hit one of the twin towers in Manhattan ! We remained glued to the screen, following the subsequent tragic developments : the plane crashing on the Pentagon, the dramatic, spectacular collapse of the two towers, the crash of the fourth plane near Pittsburgh, the heroic rescue services who did all they could... and all of this shown live !

DENIS SASSOU NGUESSO

*— Yes, along with the political event that day, we dis-
covered a new phenomenon : the entire world was able to
watch a major historical event unfolding before its eyes in
real time. When we think about it, seeing history in the
making like a gigantic live show, with no perspective or
possibility of analysis, can be both a good and bad thing.
What do you think ? What's your opinion of the Internet,
which is, as they say, turning the whole world into a village,
and which is now part of everyday life all over the globe ?*

In itself, it's a good thing if everyone has the
same opportunity of access to what's both a
medium and a communication tool. Now, the
question we have to answer is how we can keep
control of it. How can we avoid being "devoured"
by this new technology, which isn't just mesmeri-
sing – especially for the youngest among us – but
also delivers words and pictures that can sometimes be dangerous ? How can we regulate it to
avoid becoming its victim tomorrow ? Don't
forget that anyone can write whatever they like
about you anonymously on the Internet and their
message will travel round the world and be read
by millions of people. That's the risk. Netsurfers
are in permanent danger of being manipulated and
exposed to every form of disinformation. Failing
to recognise this problem shows a lack of responsibility. Like me, over the last few years, you've
heard of more and more young people in the
United States and Europe storming their school or
university with weapons and killing their class-

174

mates and teachers. All have previously left a message on the Internet ; all of them have been filmed with the weapons they had in their possession. If there were no possibility of putting on a show, of reaching an audience, would there be so many of these young murderers ? I think we have to ask ourselves that question seriously.

— *But if you ask that, you're in danger of being seen as a censor !*

We have to stop this sanctimoniousness and new orthodoxy ! If there's a problem – and on the question we're discussing, there *is* a problem – we have to ask how, in certain cases, we can go about limiting access to certain sites. It's not a crime to ask that ! What are we afraid of ? In passing, I'd like to point out that not only are the media totally free in the Congo, they're protected by law : the press cannot be prosecuted !

— *How healthy is the opposition press in the Congo ?*

90 % of the Congolese press is in opposition.

— *How did the Congolese feel about Barack Obama's arrival in the White House, President ?*

I think everyone felt the occasion would undoubtedly be among the most important events of this century. That Obama, an African American, has come to power elected by a majority of white people is a qualitative change. It can even be read as a true plebiscite from all the components of American society : Latin Americans, Whites of every origin, Blacks and Native Americans. It was an extraordinary event that we witnessed in November 2008 !

— Do you think that Obama will change US policy significantly, especially towards Africa ?

I don't really think so. The fact that he's an African American won't suddenly make him favour Africa. I don't believe that. He's primarily there to protect the interests of the people of the United States of America. That's why he was elected. His project is for America. We shouldn't delude ourselves about that. However, we have to admit that in a country that racially discriminated against its black community less than a century ago, this is suddenly a great leap forward !

— So the rather wild enthusiasm that greeted his election around the world, especially in Africa, will probably die down over the coming months ?

The whole world welcomed Barack Obama's victory and that enthusiasm was justified ! In just a few months, we've seen him make significant changes in certain areas of American policy : the announcement of a progressive withdrawal of

American troops from Iraq according to a precise schedule, a declared intention to reopen talks with Syria and even Iran, the closure of the Guantanamo prison camp and the interventionist economic and financial policy of his administration in dealing with the economic crisis. That's already quite a list! I hope the people who've been so enthusiastic about the start of his term won't be disappointed.

– PART THREE –

– 23 –

RUMOURS AND DEFAMATION

NGOs manipulated – Libel and
lies – The reasons for a hate campaign

*– How do you view NGOs and their work in Africa ?
You seem quite critical of them ;*

First, you have to remember that these are non-governmental associations that have basically declared themselves necessary. They have no actual legitimacy, they haven't been elected : they and they alone have decided that they ought to carry out this or that initiative in one sector or another. It's important to understand that. Obviously, the goals that most of them have set themselves are noble and their action in the field is often efficacious. However, not all these organisations are necessary, useful or effective. Some even misuse their rights, treating developing nations as vassal states and blithely ignoring their own ethical principles as they go. Others, inten-

181

tionally or not, become tools for the advancement of various interests.

— You've said that some NGOs are manipulated by vulture funds. First, what are these funds ?

They're funds from the Anglo-Saxon world that buy up the debt of African nations in difficulty at bargain prices and then demand that these nations repay the sums a hundred times over ! We've taken action against these funds. Our problem's resolved now, but in the meantime, they've waged a vast, lethal campaign of destabilisation against us.

— In other words, these funds work hand in hand with some rather dubious NGOs.

Yes, NGOs that spread rumours and maintain networks that verge on the subversive, which in turn manipulate media with few scruples and an insatiable appetite for sensational claims, which they repeat without even attempting to find out whether they're true or not.

— You say it's these NGOs that have fed false allegations about you and your family to the press, allegations that certain media have passed on without even bothering to check the facts ? Basically, these media felt justified in claiming that you had a hundred foreign bank accounts and a number of properties in France. Is it true ?

It's untrue, completely untrue! I've never concealed what I own and I don't see why I would! I have a three to four-room apartment on the second floor of a building in avenue Rapp in Paris. Hundreds of people, Congolese and others, have visited me there. They can confirm what I say. I mainly received visitors there when I was in Paris from 1995 to 1997, during my "wilderness years". Then a lot of foolishness has been written about my house in Le Vésinet, in the Yvelines. It's next to a railway line and was totally rundown when I bought it in 1983. Since then, I've renovated it, but it's still no chateau, that's for sure! When I bought it, my children lived there while they were studying in Paris, then I lent it to sick relations who were in France for treatment, before turning it into a stopover place for my fellow citizens. Actually, it was a lot of trouble as a stopover, with heating, water, electricity and maintenance issues. Unbelievably, some NGOs have made that property out to be a palace! The fact that certain media have repeated this preposterous claim is outrageous! It certainly raises serious doubts about the quality of some journalists' work. Why didn't they come and check? Why didn't they ask me? It wouldn't have been difficult. I would have been completely open with them. Yet they prefer to depict the President of the Republic of the Congo as an odious person who creams off the wealth of his country for his personal gain. Now if that isn't subversion on the part of these NGOs, aimed at destroying a people's morale and encouraging insurrection, what is it ?

— How did you respond to the accusations about the bank accounts you were said to hold abroad ?

In the simplest way possible. I asked the French banks who have accounts in my name to publish a list of the hundred and twelve accounts the press has alleged I have in France. I asked that.

— And so far, you've seen nothing.

There's still been no response. Yet when there was some trial or other, they managed to publish details of President Bongo's accounts in just twenty-four hours. I'm still waiting.

— Don't you think that journalists lump you together with President Bongo, given your close relationship ?

Bongo's Bongo and Sassou's Sassou ! They can talk about one without necessarily having to talk about the other, and vice versa !

— Are you thinking of taking legal action ?

Some of my staff have advised me to sue for libel. I'm not planning to do so for the moment. But when the time comes, I reserve the right to defend my name if necessary.

— What would you say to those people who criticise some of your children for their excesses ?

Any children can be guilty of excesses, whoever they are. Once they're adults, they must be held responsible for their own behaviour. That's clear and unarguable. Parents aren't in any way responsible for what their adult children may do, since those children are adults and living their own lives. That's their right limited only by the law, which is exactly the same for all. Judging them isn't the same thing as judging their parents.

— You've also been criticised for the cost of your foreign trips.

Why ? When the President of the Congo attends a session of the United Nations General Assembly in New York to represent his country, can't he stay in a better class of hotel such as the *Waldorf Astoria*, like any other head of state, including President Bush ? Where do you think I should stay because I'm an African ? In a hotel in Harlem or a bed and breakfast in the Bronx ? Don't I have the right to stay there at my country's expense ? In fact, has anyone asked the Congolese what they think ? After all, it directly concerns them, rather than anyone else. Someone should ask them where they want their President to stay in these cases. These NGOs should stop lecturing the whole world all the time. In fact, don't you think this lecturing reveals a strangely neo-colonialist attitude ? What right do some people think they have to drag the names of their fellow human beings through the mud ? In what name ? In whose name ?

Anyway, to finish with this subject and perhaps draw some conclusions, now we have the Internet and the global village we mentioned earlier, and now that everyone is informed of everything instantly, whether it's true or false, I can see a genuine danger in this kind of manipulation. Disinformation can harm a State and its president, a group, a company or a private individual. How can they defend themselves ? If a fabrication appears on the Web, we can't stop it and obviously any denial we make won't have the same impact. If the fabrication is believed and so becomes "credible", even just for a few hours, you can publish all the refutations you want, it won't do you any good. There'll always be someone to claim there's no smoke without fire.

Sadly, there are plenty of examples of this. The most famous is to do with the 11th September 2001. Certain individuals actually felt they could claim that no plane had crashed into the Pentagon ! That claim went all around the world. It was repeated and commented and enlarged on, and gradually made credible, especially by those who hoped to make political capital out of it. Even today, despite the proof that's been provided, thousands of people are still convinced that no plane crashed into the American Department of Defense !

— The last accusation levelled against you is the "Braz-zaville Beach" affair. In April and May 1999, during the civil war, your militia are accused of having massacred more than three hundred and fifty people who were trying to return to the Congo from Kinshasa. Legal proceedings are in progress.

Like the previous accusations, this is part of a campaign of disinformation and manipulation directed against the Congo and its President. As you can imagine, if this alleged "massacre" had really taken place, remains would have been found. Many families would have been in mourning and there would have been floating bodies, some of them recovered downstream. Yet there were no reports of any of that. There were even claims that pyres had been built !

An opponent of the Congolese government who'd left the country said he'd seen clouds of smoke through the window of his office before leaving Brazzaville. He concluded that they came from burning bodies ! But where was the proof of all that ? Where ? The Congolese who'd gone into exile in Kinshasa returned safely in a special operation organised with the help of the United Nations High Commission for Refugees. A tripartite agreement was negotiated for the purpose between the governments of Brazzaville and Kinshasa and the HCR.

In any case, there was a trial over the "Beach" affair, which was broadcast live – yes, live ! – on radio and television. It lasted more than a month and the court had the opportunity to question all the accused, whatever their office or rank. At no point in the trial did anyone produce even the slightest evidence of any "massacre" ! Simply claiming something isn't enough, you have to show it happened. This disinformation was actually a part of the same campaign of manipulation.

– How do you explain why you're the target of this kind of attack ? What do you think is behind this desire to damage your reputation ?

A desire to damage my reputation and a desire to destabilise an entire country ! Behind the NGOs and other so-called champions of human rights are a number of Congolese in exile, the very ones who sparked the violence in our country before fleeing abroad and taking refuge in Paris and other places. What's more, they've found allies and resources in the shape of the "vulture funds" we mentioned, who share their aim : to encourage the population of the Congo to rebel and destabilise its government.

– When you explain that to journalists, how do they react ? Do they understand your denials ?

The most honest journalists, the ones who genuinely investigate allegations – and they're one and the same – realise how crude a manipulation this is. As for the rest obviously, there are none so blind as those who will not see !

– 24 –

POWER

Counsel and solitude –
Ho Chi Minh and de Gaulle

– Perhaps we can talk a little about you, President. You'll soon have been in power in the Congo for twenty-five years in two separate periods. After twenty-five years, do you still have the same enthusiasm and energy you started out with?

I'm as determined as ever to serve my people and country. While a politician may be physically less vigorous at sixty-six or sixty-seven than thirty years before, that doesn't affect their commitment, the goals they've set themselves or their desire to serve. You find energy in the idea you have of your people and country, and in the memory of where you're from and how far you've come. I'm the expression of this country's land and its people. Those of our generation who are now in positions of responsibility have come a very long way. Others today are still where we once were and they must be guided along the path, helped to make progress. We have to move forward, making sure that everyone without exception has the chance to enjoy a decent life tomorrow.

— *What does being in power mean to you ? The power to lead, to build, to help ? How would you define it ?*

For me, the exercise of power primarily means moving things in the right direction. Then it means making choices and decisions, and obviously taking responsibility for them. It is one of our duties to provide hope and providing hope means rallying the people round ideas and initiatives, convincing them to advance together towards a common goal. Without those things, power is power for power's sake, and in that case, it's of no benefit. Worse, it poses a threat.

— *Power also involves great solitude, of course.*

Obviously, you're surrounded by a large staff and all these people are essential : their work, advice and comments are necessary. Nothing could be achieved without them. Even so, in certain circumstances, you can suddenly be filled with a feeling of great solitude. This is always at a time when you have to make a final decision. You've listened to everyone, read all the arguments and grasped all the analyses, and now it's up to you to make the right decision in all conscience and for the sole benefit of those who trust in you. There can be no regrets or remorse. We know that tomorrow, we'll have to answer to our people and to history. That's when we feel great solitude. Yet I believe that we also draw strength from those moments.

— Could you give us an example ?

Yes. It didn't involve me, it involved Marien Ngouabi. On that occasion, the people were furious. They were demanding he condemn one of the country's politicians to death. The situation was explosive and the public pressure huge. Ngouabi decided to think about it overnight. Actually, I don't think he got any sleep. The next day, he announced his decision. He told the enraged population, who were still demanding the accused be put to death immediately, that the man wouldn't be executed. I don't think anyone was so alone that night as the President of the Congo !

— Earlier on, you mentioned your staff and praised their self-denial and hard work, but aren't you sometimes the hostage of your own staff ?

They may sometimes be tempted to wrap their chief up in a cocoon. That's been known to happen. You have to be aware of that possibility and takes steps to prevent it.

— How do you escape what you call a "cocoon"?

Well, it hasn't happened to me, but if there were an attempt of this kind, it wouldn't be hard to stay in touch with the people. You simply have to go out and meet them. I very often do just that. In fact, I'd say it's a genuine necessity for me, like the air I breathe.

— In any body of staff providing support for a personality — especially one holding the highest office in a country — there are sometimes ferocious struggles for influence. Everyone wants to be as close as possible to the light. Then there are people who try to take advantage of their position in one way or another, sometimes bending the law to breaking point. Are you aware of this or don't you think the phenomenon exists among your staff?

Decision-makers are always surrounded by intrigues and the dealings of interest groups. Since the dawn of time, every court, palace and entourage has had its share of scheming and machinations. Any responsible leader will be aware of this and ensure that the phenomenon isn't allowed to get out of hand, since there's a risk it will gradually corrupt everything around it.

— There's no question of your leaving for the time being, but do you sometimes think about your retirement?

I have to say I never think about it. However, there's already been an interval between my terms of office as Head of State. At the time, I returned to my village and remained busy. If my successor had left me alone, I might have stayed there. In any case, I don't generally think about my personal future too far ahead.

— Do you have special references in world history ? "Symbolic people", you might say ?

Not necessarily. I do admire Ho Chi Minh, but the patriot rather than the communist leader, the man who served his people for love of his country. For the same reason, I'd include General de Gaulle in this personal pantheon, a man who was also driven by patriotism to battle to the end, stand up to the powerful and confront hatred, and who suffered public ingratitude at least twice.

— Of course, Ho Chi Minh and de Gaulle were fighting men.

Fighting men and men of conviction !

THE CONGO
FOR THE ENVIRONMENT

– You apparently have a love of nature and of trees in particular, President.

Well, my region – the Congo basin – is seen as the world's second "ecological lung" after the Amazon. Our territory is home to several thousand plant species and several hundred mammal and bird species. Remember the Congo has a network of national parks and reserves covering an area of more than 3.6 million hectares – more than 11 % of the country's total surface area, quite a large share ! That's why we intend to play our part in the battle currently waged almost everywhere in the world against global warming and the destruction of ecosystems. In 2005, I organised the 2nd Summit of Heads of State for the Conservation and Sustainable Management of Forest Ecosystems in Central Africa. The meeting was held in

Brazzaville[1], because I felt there was a need to co-ordinate the different initiatives adopted by countries concerned about the future of the Congo basin. At this summit, which was attended by United Nations Secretary-General Kofi Annan, we voted in favour of a plan of action which won the full support of the international community. In 2008, I also organised the Sixth World Forum on Sustainable Development in Brazzaville[2].

— *What do the 3.6 million hectares of protected zones in the Congo actually hold ?*

Nature ! A nature that's been entirely, fully conserved. There are no industrial facilities, no logging operations, no hunting... nothing whatsoever that might harm the ecosystem in any way.

— *How did the Congolese become aware of these environmental issues ?*

They've been environmentally aware for a long time. As early as the Sixties, the Congo regulated logging in its forests – 22 million hectares in all – and began reforestation operations. I should point out that ecological concerns weren't yet an issue at that time and some international bodies – quite

---

1. See appendix IV.
2. See appendix V.

important ones – were more inclined to urge us to "skim off the cream" of our southern forests, advice we fortunately didn't follow. To offer an even more practical example in answer to your question, let me point out that a Congolese law voted on my initiative requires each citizen to plant a fruit or forest tree once a year. So every year – on the 6th November to be precise – we have Tree Day. On that day, wherever they are in the country, the Congolese must plant a tree.

– Does that mean that every Congolese citizen plants a tree every year ?

That's the law and ignorance of the law is no defence, as you know. I'm not saying that every Congolese citizen plants a tree, but it's the law. Sometimes it's a very organised social event. Some prefects set up group planting sessions, teachers do the same with their classes, and so on.

– Do they decide where to plant the trees ?

No, the locations are chosen by experts, who also recommend the species to be planted.

– Do you have a favourite tree ? You mention the mango tree in the title of your last book.

It may disappoint you, but I don't prefer any one particular tree, probably because I'm equally fond of them all.

– 26 –

"A SOUND MIND
IN A SOUND BODY"

– There's a very striking aspect of the Congo with its relatively small population : the profusion of artistic activities – painting, literature, drama, music and dancing. Why is that ?

Like you, I've noticed that phenomenon and it fills me with a great sense of satisfaction and pride. Frankly, though, I can't explain it. It must be in the Congolese nature. The only other reason I can suggest is the very high level of school attendance in our country, which reached 100 % a few years ago. Given the events that followed, the figure fell slightly, but is now rising sharply again.

– You're a sports enthusiast, President. What's your favourite sport ?

I was very athletic when I was younger. I've practised many sports – team sports, such as basketball and football, as well as individual sports, such as tennis and table tennis. The army introduced me to horse riding. I loved to ride ! I also did a lot of parachute jumping in the army, of course. Today, I swim a lot, but my favourite spectator sports are football and tennis.

– Do you support a particular football team ?

Chiefly the Congo football team, of course, even though it's not at its best today. It did win the African Cup of Nations in 1972, though. The Congo is seen as a footballing nation in Africa. Today, the national squad's competitive level is low and we're working to improve it. Apart from my own country's team, since 1958, I've been supporting Brazil because of Pelé, and Real Madrid because of Di Stefano.

– Have you met Pelé ?

Yes, he came to play here in the Congo twice.

– Africa has a problem with football : the drain of its best players to Europe. That means its national champions-hips are far below their natural level.

That's true. But football has been turned into an industry. Players are bought like equipment today. Money has taken over the sport. What can we do ?

— It also means that Africa is finding it increasingly hard to hold onto its athletes.

As are other countries, in Europe, for instance. Look at the French team. Most of its players compete in foreign championships, in England, Italy, Spain or Germany. Brazil and Argentina also face increasing demand for their players, who are going to Europe too. That's why the Confederation of African Football has made a decision I feel is important and deserving of encouragement. Along with the African Cup of Nations, a competition where players remaining in Africa or playing abroad compete in their national teams, it now organises another continent-wide competition : the African Nations Championship. Only players who compete in their national championship all year round can play in it.

— As a way of encouraging new talent ?

Absolutely. It's a very good way of developing football within the continent, away from purely financial circuits.

– 27 –

SOLIDARITY IN ACTION

— Looking at how you live, President, it's obvious that your family's extremely important to you.

Family is a major part of life. In Africa, we all have large families – much broader ones than in Europe, where some people actually now regret their destruction. You once had large families too, but modern life and new types of relationship between the young and the elderly have gradually put an end to them. I think that's a pity. The family's a sanctuary, a place where we can return to our roots, share and discuss, a place where we can talk to each other frankly, a place where solidarity's not an empty word when we're confronted by distress or adversity.

— Of course, you have your wife by your side, President, playing an active part in public life in the Congo.

People often say that behind a great man, there's a great woman, and I think that's clearly true. My wife plays a very important role at my side in both private and public life. She runs a humanitarian foundation, Congo Assistance, which helps disabled children, widows and the elderly. At the same time, she organises committees to combat AIDS, working with international organisations that are fighting this scourge. She also plays an active part in the First Ladies of Africa organisation, battling drepanocytosis, sickle-cell disease, a disorder that affects African children in particular. Working with the wife of the President of Senegal, Mrs. Wade, she has fought for this disease to be recognised as a pandemic by the United Nations, so that the same resources can be devoted to its prevention and treatment as for other pandemics. The question is currently being examined in New York.

— When you mention the scourge of AIDS, what do you think about what Pope Benedict XVI had to say when he claimed that not only could the problem of AIDS not be solved by the distribution of condoms, but their use would "aggravate" the problem ?

I'd simply say this : in the Congo, we strongly encourage use of the condom. In fact, we even officially promote it.

Apart from that, we're actively taking part in a programme of education, training and prevention with UNAIDS. We've also decided to supply testing and antiretroviral drugs free of charge and make screening centres available throughout the country.

In the health domain, our initiatives are obviously not limited to the fight against AIDS. In our campaign against malaria, we've introduced free care for pregnant women and for children from birth to the age of fifteen, as well as the distribution of treated mosquito nets all over the country.

– PART FOUR –

– 28 –

"LA NOUVELLE ESPÉRANCE" :
NEW HOPE

— President, in July, you're standing for re-election by your fellow-citizens. On that occasion, you'll ask them to express their trust in you once again and elect you for another term as President of the Republic of the Congo.

We're now familiar with your career and record, and perhaps we also know you a little better. For the first time, you've allowed us a glimpse of the private person. Despite your characteristic reserve, you've readily agreed to answer my questions, which haven't necessarily all been easy to answer. You've done so calmly and with an obvious wish to speak frankly.

I now suggest we look to the future and the plans you're suggesting for the Congo over the next seven years.

Your manifesto is entitled, "La Nouvelle Espérance : Le Chemin d'Avenir" (New Hope : The Path of the Future). Why ?

"New Hope" was the name I gave to the social programme I presented to my fellow citizens in

211

2002, which a very large majority of them approved. Thanks to this New Hope, the Congo is today enjoying peace and security. Once more, everything is possible in our country. Our prospects, obscured by a period of blood and ashes, have grown brighter. The hope of a better future has taken shape. Stifled yesterday, the expectation of a better life is blooming again. Since 2002, we've re-laid the foundations of a respectable, respected sovereign nation, carefully paving the way for a state of law, an economy tending towards diversification and modernisation, and a peaceful, safe, stable society enjoying renewed harmony and emergent solidarity. We've begun the job of knitting together the entire country with a basic infrastructure. We've started to clear State debts in agreement with the Bretton Woods institutions, and continued to reform the national financial system. We've worked on sub-regional integration and the position and influence of the Congo on the international scene.

– Of course, the Congo was in a critical state...

Yes. The work we did was essential in a country that was on the verge of imploding, a disordered country that had lost all faith in itself, which needed the reasons and means to hope again. We did that work with the people of the Congo, all of us together. Now we must continue to work together, with an eye to continuity and consistency, so that there's no split, fracture or fragmentation of our essential choices, fundamental projects or collective progress towards the realisation of our shared destiny.

— *So what new ambitions have you included in your manifesto for the next seven years ?*

The priority is to modernise and industrialise the country. That has to be the core of the mobilisation programme for the years 2009-2016, the "path of the future" leading to development, increased well-being and a better quality of life for one and all.

— *So "The Path of the Future" is the title of this programme that you're presenting to the Congolese, a programme that follows on from the "New Hope" programme.*

Absolutely. The continuity and new impetus that characterise the "Path of the Future" converge towards a single, powerful goal : to turn the Congo into a radically different country by 2016, a modernised, attractive nation, a major producer of goods and provider of services, a competitive, creative country, properly integrated within its international sub-region and the world.

A MODERNISED CONGO

— Now that we've talked about the overall nature of the programme and its governing principles, perhaps we can look at its actual content. First of all, its core element, which, as you said earlier on, is the country's modernisation.

We've chosen six areas where we'll apply our modernisation efforts : infrastructure, community life, public economic governance, the civil service, the armed forces and police, and finally political life and foreign relations.

— Let's start with infrastructure. Can you perhaps give some examples of actual initiatives ?

Actual initiatives ? Well, at least 2,000 billion CFA francs will be invested in physically modernising our country over the next seven years. If the Congolese again express their trust in me, by the end of my next term of office, electricity will be available throughout the country. There'll be a

permanent power supply in all provincial administrative centres, towns and urban areas at least.
Similarly, all towns will have drinking water on tap.
Finally, there'll be new transportation corridors to
permanently open up certain regions : projects will
be implemented to construct highways, railway
lines and airports, and develop waterways.

— *Turning to the next area, I suppose that modernising
community life means giving a boost to education, employment and health.*

Yes, we'll be working on all those concerns,
along with the environment, new technologies,
culture and sport. However, our goals also include
tackling high prices and corruption, and especially
providing qualification-oriented training. Indeed,
we can only achieve results if we succeed in training young people at every level and in every field,
helping them to obtain the necessary qualifications.

— *Can you give us a specific example in relation to these
issues ?*

Yes. In fact, I'll give you three. First, we're going
to ask Parliament to expedite the examination of
a bill to change employment law. In future, we'd
like all companies established or beginning to do
business in the Congo to give priority to hiring
unemployed Congolese workers. The second proposal is related to health. Over the next seven-year

term, we're committed to building a public general hospital in each regional administrative centre and in towns with a population of more than 50,000. Each regional administrative centre will be equipped with a medium-sized hospital and one to three clinics, depending on the size of the region. In villages of more than 1,000 inhabitants, we'll build an integrated health centre that will operate all year round. Finally, my last concrete example is the end of the wage freeze at the start of the next seven-year presidential term.

– *Why wasn't this decided before ?*

The priority task was to restore macroeconomic and financial balance through the IMF and World Bank Poverty Reduction and Growth Facility (PRGF) programme, which we are currently implementing. It should be completed this year.

– *Another area of this vast modernisation programme : public economic governance.*

The private sector has proved to be of limited efficacy as the main player in development in the Congo and elsewhere, and the current crisis of capitalism also reveals its anomalies on a global level. In any case, no private sector can launch and lastingly maintain large-scale industrial or agricultural development programmes in our country, so it's primarily up to the State to act, which is ultimately as it should be. It's the State that will encourage different companies to develop their activity and thrive in one sector or another, offering assistance if necessary. It's the State that will strive to attract reliable, experienced private investors to the country and found mixed enterprises with them.

— So those will be the respective roles of the State and private companies. What are your plans for the financial system ?

The State will have to involve itself directly in the organisation of the appropriate financial mechanisms for different sectors of vital importance. It will also set up regional investment and development funds to promote investment in each region of the country. If possible, the State will also participate as a minority shareholder in the setting-up of banks specialised in funding farming, industry, public works, trade, etc.

— Moving on to the civil service...

The civil service has to move with the times. That's why we intend to computerise it fully over the next seven years. A plan will be adopted to that end. We also want to make life easier for the Congolese. There'll be a reform of all administrative procedures applied since independence and still in force. They must be adapted to our modern society and, above all, simplified.

– What does modernising the armed forces and police imply in real terms ?

It firstly means that all elements of our army, as well as the gendarmerie and police, must be equipped with material that corresponds to international norms. It also means introducing more effective methods of training and commanding soldiers and police officers. That and other initiatives that would take too long to describe here in detail will be included in seven-year programme legislation to be presented to Parliament at the start of the new seven-year term.

– 30 –

ENHANCED DIALOGUE

– The last area of planned modernisation is national political life and foreign relations. If you agree, President, perhaps we can examine the political domain first.

In the political domain, we'll be organising an extensive consultation of the nation by 2012 to examine a new electoral law to govern the organisation of different elections in future. We promise that everything will be done to ensure that the constitutional election calendar is scrupulously observed and that all elections are organised in conditions of freedom and total openness. From the new school year of 2010-2011, civic education lessons will be compulsory in the country's secondary schools. I think you'll agree that these are tangible measures.

– Yes. But does this programme also include initiatives to strengthen the role of the opposition ?

DENIS SASSOU NGUESSO

A number of initiatives, actually. We'll be talking
to the opposition and listening to its advice, working with it to define the specific rights it will enjoy
in Parliament and on regional and local councils.
A bill will be drawn up. Once the law is introduced, the opposition will be able to chair one or
more parliamentary committees and hold one or
more posts on regional and municipal council
committees. In the same spirit of dialogue, we
intend to hold systematic talks with the opposition,
associations and representatives of civil society
before any programmes or bills are brought before
Parliament on issues such as citizenship, nationa-
lity or the exercise of public freedoms. We'll also
follow the same procedure of dialogue with the
opposition before negotiating any international
treaties or agreements liable to affect the exercise
of national sovereignty. Finally – and this is an
important point – we wish to introduce funding
for political parties.

– 31 –

A PROMISING FUTURE
FOR THE REGION

— Earlier on, you mentioned foreign relations.

You know the importance I attach to the development of international sub-regional groups with
a view to uniting our continent step by step. In
fact, we've talked about that subject at length in
this interview. Over the next seven years, I'd like
the Congo to work on revitalising the Economic
Community of Central African States.

— Could you be more specific ?

Yes. Primarily by focusing on the achievement
of joint major projects in the fields of transport,
energy, natural-resource management and training
and research. An example in the field of energy
would be to re-examine the renovation and exten-
sion of the Inga dam and its power lines supplying
the region. Another example, in the field of

research, would be to set up regional centres of excellence for agronomy and the application of new technologies. Those are the kinds of partnership that can be formed with our neighbours. Finally, as you know, the world is increasingly governed by the economy – a phenomenon that has recently been confirmed by the global impact of the ongoing economic crisis – so we'd like to strengthen the economic sections of our diplomatic missions, especially to economically powerful countries. They'll be required to act as "fund-hunters", attracting investors to the Congo who can actively participate in the development of our country.

– 32 –

NECESSARY INDUSTRIALISATION

– So modernisation in all its different aspects was the first major component of your programme.

Yes, the Congo has to play an active part in the development process. This means organising the mass production of goods and even services. We'll also need to ensure high growth of national wealth and employment.

– In concrete terms ?

Well, for instance, the State must encourage the development of industry – or develop it itself if necessary – to harvest and process the country's natural resources, producing consumer goods and equipment after research into the potential of both domestic and regional markets. I insist on the regional aspect, since – let me repeat this – we must increasingly plan our development on a regional level. Obviously, I'm not only referring to

the industrial domain. In time, the Economic
Community of Central African States, which has
a population of a hundred and twenty-two million
consumers today, is bound to form a great single
market. Its population will undoubtedly number
an impressive hundred and fifty million by 2016 !
That's why the Congo must position itself in this
great community today.

— *Coming back to industrial development, what specific
sectors will be involved ?*

Agri-foodstuffs, of course – that's a priority –
but also the processing of marine and forest
resources. Other sectors will obviously include oil
and its by-products, mining, and so on.

— *Agriculture is a major factor in your industrialisation
programme.*

As we've already mentioned, only 2 % of Congolese territory is farmed. That's a ludicrous figure !
We have to make our soil more profitable. So the
Congolese must return to the countryside. Now,
if we're to persuade them to do this, we can't ask
them to work the land as their ancestors did. We
have to mechanise our farming and excite interest
among young people by offering suitable training.
We must then ensure a synergy between agriculture and industry. The production of a well-orga-
nised, dynamic, prolific farming sector should lead

to the development of agri-foodstuffs and bioe-
nergy industries.

*— In your previous programme, you spoke of the creation
of special economic zones in certain regions of the Congo
— what we might call "free-trade zones". Where do things
stand today ?*

The initiative had to be rescheduled because the
research begun on these special economic zones
wasn't complete. So we plan to implement the project over the next seven years.

— Could you be more precise ?

These special economic zones or SEZs will be
located on the banks of the Sangha to the north,
on the banks of the Alima in the centre, on the
banks of the Congo river to the southeast and on
the Atlantic coast to the southwest. The SEZs will
provide a focus for industries specialised in products for export. They'll enjoy sufficiently attractive
tax incentives to encourage many companies to do
business there. Our objective is for the exportable
products of the Likouala and Sangha regions to be
processed in the Sangha SEZ. The exportable products of the Cuvette, Cuvette-Ouest and Plateaux
regions will go to the Alima SEZ and those of the
Pool and Brazzaville regions to the Congo river
SEZ. Finally, the production of the Bouenza,
Lékoumou, Niari, Kouilou and Pointe-Noire
regions will be processed in the Atlantic SEZ.

– 33 –

A WELCOMING CONGO

— *The Congo has tremendous potential for tourism with its forests, rivers, fauna and huge nature reserves, not to mention its great cultural wealth – music, dancing, painting and crafts. It seems surprising that it doesn't attract more tourists. Now the country is totally secure again, what plans do you have for this economically promising sector ?*

Since the tragic events here, we've obviously been unable to tackle the question of tourism. Our priority has been to get the economy moving again, put our finances in order and bring security to every part of the country. Now we've achieved that, we must of course work to develop one of the Congo's great resources : tourism, an industry that creates local jobs. That's why we anticipate the State investing more in the development of tourist centres over the coming years, by the Atlantic Ocean and inland too, in areas chosen for their attractions. Obviously, we'll also be developing ecotourism in the protected parts of our country.

— Will you encourage the development of the cultural and artistic activities we mentioned earlier, which flourish in your country ?

The State will make all the necessary efforts to showcase our national culture and arts to the full, along with our country's historic sites. Private investment will be encouraged, especially for the construction of major hotels and leisure centres.

— How do you plan to organise this full-scale revival of tourism in the Congo ?

If our programme is approved by the Congolese, this year, in 2009, we'll set up an office for the promotion of the tourist industry. Among its other tasks, this body will be responsible for attracting tour operators to our country to invest here, and also for seeking funding from multilateral institutions – the World Bank, the UNDP, et cetera – to back our tourism-development programme.

— With what financial goals ?

Our aim is for tourism to make up more than 10 % of the Congo's GNP in seven years' time.

THE "PATH OF THE FUTURE"

— So to conclude, if you're re-elected, your priority will be to focus on the modernisation and industrialisation of the country.

I can't stress my determination to modernise and industrialise the Congo enough ! It's based on my intention to transform the country, secure it a place among the new emergent nations and radically renovate our society to make it closer-knit and more open and tranquil. I want to see a Congo where everyone has an opportunity for complete fulfilment. What's more important to me than anything else is our country's progress and the happiness of its people. Those are prospects within our grasp. To achieve them, we have to turn away from the path of accident and imprecision, and take a safer, more reliable path : the "Path of the Future".

– APPENDICES –

Over the following pages, I was keen to include a few texts that are particularly important to me.

The first is "J'assume" (I Accept Responsibility), my message to all the Congolese on the 26th April 1991 as our country faced the first throes of a major crisis that would do it lasting damage.

The subsequent extracts are taken from the speech I gave to the OAU in Addis Ababa on the 28th July 1986 as I was preparing to take office as its President. They deal with the need for African unity and the struggle against apartheid.

The third text is from the opening speech of the international "Writers Against Apartheid" conference we organised in Brazzaville in May 1987.

Finally, I have added two extracts from speeches about sustainable development that I gave at two international meetings organised in Brazzaville in 2005 and 2008. I felt it was essential that they should feature in this book, since my country lies at the heart of the Congo basin, seen as the world's second "ecological lung" after the Amazon basin.

– I –

« J'ASSUME »
(I ACCEPT RESPONSIBILITY)

Message to the Nation from
the President of the Republic of the Congo
(Brazzaville, 26th April 1991)

People of the Congo...
My dear fellow citizens...

Since the 25th February last, a momentous event has been taking place : the National Conference, responsible for shaping the new face of our country.

The sometimes vehement discussions held there and the often virulent words spoken reflect a thirst for expression after more than a quarter of a century of the single-party system.

However, the significant fact is that, for the first time, we are preparing to introduce radical changes peacefully and responsibly, with no bloodshed or violence.

That is a victory over ourselves.

What is happening across the continent should encourage us to continue down this path. Total freedom of expression reigns both in the conference hall of the Palais des Congrès and outside.

Each participant contributes according to their temperament and education. I have often observed a great deal of lucidity, sometimes excess and emotion, but always a love of our country.

And that is what counts.

Today, I would like to draw a few brief conclusions from this experience and also talk about our country's future.

I will begin by examining the great lessons of history learned from thirty years of independence, underlining the fact that the reprehensible behaviour of the past has not been limited to a single man, tribe, region, country or continent.

I will then stress the significance of the National Conference – a collective purification – and the goal it must achieve – national reconciliation.

Finally, I will speak of all the reasons for hope provided by the discussions of the National Conference, the conditions needed for our development and the prospect of a better future that we now enjoy.

People of the Congo...

Daughters and sons of this country have decided to re-examine our recent past. They have identified failings and many areas of uncertainty. They have rightly condemned the violence, which we all abhor. For too long, that violence lay at the heart of every system and was all too often the sole method of taking power. They have also condemned misuse of our national resources, social inequality and unacceptable behaviour, the whole aim here being to exorcise the demons of this rather inglorious past and introduce new values.

People of the Congo...

It is my belief that we should refrain from rewriting our common history to suit current circumstances.

The historical events that occurred in our country in August 1963, July 1968 and February 1979 can be justified in the context of the time. They have been assessed in different ways by different speakers.

Together, we must accept these developments. We must stop wallowing in a past that divides us and turn to the present... and, even more, the future.

Despite its acknowledged progress – as various achievements show, today's Congo is no longer the country it was in 1960 – from every viewpoint – political, economic, social and cultural – our nation still remains to be built.

Excesses and waste have been deplored. In this vast enterprise of national construction, mistakes and faults have been inevitable and have undeniably occurred. We have to recognise this. Indeed, our previous speeches have always called on our fellow citizens to adopt a better spirit and attitude in relation to values of work, justice and solidarity.

In our country, officials from all political backgrounds and regions have failed in their duty.

When a farmer or worker suffers from a lack of security, this does not reflect their tribal or regional colour.

People of the Congo...

There has been much mention of painful, tragic passages in our recent history. Many of our country's children have perished, victims of conflicts specific to the systems we have known.

Some have paid for our mistakes with their blood, while others have died because they took up arms against the Republic. Public accounts relating to some of these still obscure episodes have thrown new light on events. Others have been examined in the course of court proceedings whose verdicts can only be challenged if new evidence is brought.

Dear fellow citizens...

What is the meaning of this National Conference that we all agreed on ? Its great process of introspection must first and foremost be aimed at national reconciliation and reconstruction.

We have to heal our wounds, not cause more rifts. Let us remember with compassion all those fellow citizens without exception !

May the memory of what befell them teach us to renounce such behaviour forever.

National reconciliation alone will enable our people to turn to the future. Let us foster it with sensible measures of rehabilitation and compensation. I believe and know that the Congo has the power to heal itself in a complete communion of hearts, minds and reason. Our collective destiny depends on it. Must we clamber over other bodies to achieve democracy ?

My answer is no. Obviously. No, because ultimately the basic issue is a human one, the issue of our life in society.

No, because we can never build unity or the future on discord and hatred.

The people of the Congo must look to their culture, convictions and behaviour. They must surpass themselves and examine their own actions in the light of a code of law and freedom that applies to all.

If not, everything we are condemning today will be repeated tomorrow.

Like you, I believe that the single-party system has its flaws. However, the multi-party system will not make people good in itself.

It is up to the individual, to each one of us, to change and adapt to pluralist democracy, in agreement and compliance with the law.

As Head of State, I see all those different things that have been said as commitments to reject the past with all its failings and turn to the future with new values, new ideas, new concepts and new practices.

People of the Congo...

During these discussions, the entire Congolese political class since independence has been called to account. Some of its leaders are no longer here to answer for their administration.

President Youlou did not have time to try the single-party system.

President Massamba-Débat, who led the first single-party organisation, the National Revolutionary Movement (MNR), is no longer with us. The same goes for Captain Marien Ngouabi, who founded the Congolese Party of Labour (PCT).

President Yhombi-Opango, who continued the experiment with the Party Military Committee (CMP), is no longer in power.

Only I remain today, now the latest Head of State, chosen by pluralist democracy to answer in their name for the government of our country by the single-party system.

Companions of great experience and deep conviction have told you their share of the truth and of all the good they have done. So I am alone in taking responsibility for the harm done, and I accept that responsibility, collectively and individually, in the name of all the leaders of this country who are no longer here.

I am refraining and will continue to refrain from accusing anyone. The future of democracy in the world, in Africa, in this part of Africa and the Congo, does not belong to those who claim to be innocent, pure and unstained, but to those who have the ability to adapt to this new requirement.

It is because of all these considerations that I accept responsibility, for us all, for all our past, for all that shared history with both its negative and positive results. I tell our people that even if serious mistakes were made, we were only ever moved by the best of intentions.

That is why humbly, in the name of the entire political class since independence, and personally, I would like to ask for our people's generous understanding and indulgence.

Separate the wheat from the chaff. Maintain and consolidate those things you may think hold the seeds of national unity, peace and patriotism.

Let us turn away once and for all from the spectre of division and hatred, from the justification of tribalism and the regionalism that sets tribes against each other.

I understand and forgive all those speakers who have occasionally spoken maliciously of me in their patriotic profession of faith.

For finally, they and I have faith in that most important thing, that thing that takes precedence over all others : total confidence in the future of the Congo, our country, the capacities of its people and the resources and hope of its youth.

The National Conference has entered a new phase : committee proceedings to draw up a platform that will lead, after a reasonable transition period, to the establishment of new democratic institutions elected by universal suffrage.

As the President in office, I solemnly declare in advance my support for those constructive, sensible decisions that will be liable to promote radical change for a new, modern economic and political system.

However, we must set ourselves clear goals and ensure we have the means needed.

The first of priorities must remain the economic reconstruction of the country and nation. This is what the Congolese people expect of us and it is on this point that there must be no failure.

The National Conference must not forget this.

A framework for development must be rapidly prepared and the necessary measures taken to start up the economy again. Focusing on their past through the discussions of the National Conference, the Congolese people are aware that the time is soon coming – in fact, has already come – when we must set to work again, for our children, our future and our freedom.

There remains a question that is in everyone's thoughts today : the progress of our democracy.

I approve of and support pluralism, since it is a decisive stage of progress and development.

However, after the joy, after the euphoria of a new freedom, we must not slip into bad habits of discord and inefficacy.

That is why the second priority is to establish an institutional framework that ensures the free exercise of a universally approved democracy, as well as the efficacy our country obviously needs.

So these are the two priorities we all agree on, because they are vital to our country.

Now we must build the new Congo in a spirit of national unity, peace and democracy.

Personally, I have every confidence in the maturity of our people and the participants at the National Conference, who will provide us with suitable plans to ensure that the democratic rebirth we aspire to takes place legally, peacefully and calmly.

I have confidence in this Presidium chaired by Monsignor Ernest Nkombo, who has moderated the sometimes heated discussions with verve, composure and objectivity.

I have confidence in those women and men whose wisdom and knowledge inevitably help to enhance the content of the discussions.

Lastly, I have confidence in the young people who are contributing so many ideas that reflect the hope they entertain in the future of their country.

Traditional chiefs, guardians of the values that have helped to forge our national identity, village elders whose wisdom lights the way for our rural communities, elders who live among us in the towns, I ask your help and support, so that our country, with so many eyes on it today, can proudly succeed in introducing democratic pluralism, the guarantee of a better future.

To all, I again promise security – complete security – as well as my full co-operation, so that together, in peace, tranquillity and national unity, we can lay the foundations for a new, modern Congo of development and progress, providing prosperity for all the Congolese : a land of tolerance, mutual respect and fraternity.

Long live national unity !
Long live the Republic !

Denis Sassou Nguesso

– II –

Speech to the 22nd Conference of the Heads of State and Government of the OAU (Addis Ababa, 28th July 1986)
(Extracts)

The necessary unity of Africa

(...) We stand at the crossroads. In a decade, the 20th century will come to an end. Another century will begin and, with it, we will enter the third millennium. At such a juncture, what will Africa's future be ?

Let us speak frankly : in a context of Balkanisation, the future prospects are poor indeed, despite the state of euphoria that some of our countries find themselves in today. Wishes and moral considerations aside, everyday developments teach us that the influence a State can exert in certain areas seems to depend on its economic and human potential. Also, in the present century, the requirements of modern technology are such that development demands a sizeable economic space and suitable human potential.

Given this imperative, we are working towards policies of close sub-regional co-operation with a view to future economic integration, radically and decisively changing our future.

This is a long process. Only a clearly-defined Unitarian policy with the organisations we have established acting as links and stages in a dynamic process can make them strong and vigorous. Without a clear political brief, over time, these organisations may become seeds for national individualisms or, worse, battlefields for aggravated nationalisms. None of us want that.

The struggle against apartheid

(...) It seems to me that the struggle against apartheid is the catalyst for our burst of energy. Yes, we are weak. Yes, we would be unable to solve the problem of apartheid on our own.

Think, though. Have we made every effort, mustered all our forces and adequately assisted the front-line nations, victims of the deliberate, tenacious onslaught of the Pretoria regime ?

Have we even given due consideration to the proposal made by our brother Robert Mugabe, who expressed the wish that our determination to strive for the liberation of our oppressed South-African brothers should take the form of a joint military initiative, rather than resolutions ?

Are we so sunk in weakness and resigned that

we are reduced to believing that the efforts to be made to overcome apartheid are pointless ?

Are our economic difficulties so limiting that we are sure before we begin that nothing can be done ?

We must pull ourselves together – not to denounce the Pretoria regime even more furiously, but to move against it, tirelessly and on every front. Yes, if we Africans make the struggle against apartheid a persistent trait of our diplomacy, the spearhead of our States' international relations, the essential condition of our co-operation with other nations, then the friends we have around the world, the countries we deal with, would view the South African issue differently.

By genuinely facing up to our responsibility to politically and economically isolate South Africa, we will lend greater credibility to our ambition to see the international community introduce mandatory global sanctions against the apartheid system.

If the world is convinced that our countries are ready to pay the price needed for the victory of liberty and justice in South Africa, there will be more support for our cause and greater numbers of friends and allies for our struggle. To the friends and backers of South Africa, we say that humanity is marching on towards the light and that Africa, which is waging one of its final battles today, will recognise its true allies, its true partners according to their individual behaviour.

(...) Our credibility and dignity depend on it. South Africa will not be fought with words, but with deeds. Can we hope that the African community as a whole will take a small step in the right direction over the next few months ?

More than ever, we have to break the chains that maintain us in a state of humiliation, contempt and domination.

In the current strategic game, Africa's situation is neither comfortable nor easy. We do not have force or power on our side. The iron law of international relations restrains us, but we are sure that through solidarity, tenacity and courage, we poor, deprived peoples will be able to sway the course of events and force the hand of destiny in order to achieve a new balance.

Should we, Member States of the OAU, not push ourselves a little further, take a fresh look at our ways of thinking and acting, and be moved to even greater efforts, to a greater contribution to the causes we serve, which are those of dignity, liberty and a belief in humanity ?

What can we do to restore hope to Africans who are marginalised and inoculated with despondency today ?

They must definitely be reconciled with themselves, accepting their identity and specific nature, if they are to build independent economies, and acquire and control the means to assert their full personality.

For our countries, bled white by economic crisis, debt and natural disasters, at a time when survival is the key, does this talk of assertion not suggest too distant a future for our people, still in need of everything, to grasp ?

Even so, we must urge our States to pursue this ambition, for it is at this price and this price alone that they will cease to be born victims.

The longest of journeys begins with a single step. We will owe our salvation to sustained, sustainable effort.

– III –

Opening speech
at the "Writers Against Apartheid"
International Symposium
(Brazzaville, 25th May 1987)
(Extracts)

(...) Obviously, your presence and commitment
are contributing to one of the most significant
pages in my country's history, because through
you, humanity is resisting one of the most humi-
liating violations of human dignity of our times.

All Africa, and everyone who believes that each
person has the right to the respect of others, appre-
ciates the tribute you are paying and the comfort
you are offering to those whom apartheid strives
to reduce completely to the level of subhumans.

Our first thought is for those people in that
place, recognized or anonymous heroes, spokespersons for a wounded conscience, witnesses to
an unending revolt, voices that nothing – not even
the infernal machinery of oppression – can reduce
to silence. Their tragedy, which brings us together

today, reawakens the sorrow I felt on the island of Gorée, where I saw the gates of that former hell whose stigmata remain in the world's memory five hundred years later. This is the same battle, for these are the same crimes against human beings, the same effort to dehumanise. Here, the details have no essential meaning. The basic issue is that humans are refused their human status and quality. The same struggle ? Yes. Yesterday, there was not only passivity, resignation and submissiveness, there was also revolt, resistance and refusal. Today, there is refusal and a struggle that continues every day, at every moment. (...)

Ladies and gentlemen, writers...

What do they expect of you, the oppressed of South Africa ? What do they expect of you, those men and women throughout the world who know that apartheid is a scar on Africa and a mark of shame for all ?

They expect nothing that you cannot or do not know how to do : simply your duty as writers and persons of culture. Struggling Africa, the Africa of freedom, tortured, in chains, imprisoned, downtrodden, but still standing, asks you, people of faith and mind, to increase your determination to hound this system that makes it illegal not to be racist.

Africa asks you not to grant apartheid a second's respite. There is an African proverb that says : "You don't take part in the elephant hunt by simply watching the animal's body pass by your hut".

In the words of the romantic poet Lamartine : "Shame on those who remain in their tent while the people fight for freedom".

– IV –

Opening speech at the 2nd Summit
of Heads of State on the Conservation
and Sustainable Management of Forest
Ecosystems in Central Africa
(Brazzaville, 4th-5th February 2005)
(Extract)

(...) The role played by the forest of Central Africa, a single, vast expanse of 228 million hectares, in the ecological balance of our planet, with regard to the conservation of water resources, the prevention of soil erosion, the maintenance of biodiversity, the prevention of natural risks and air cleaning, is considerable and fundamental.

The conservation and sustainable management of forest ecosystems in Central Africa, especially those of the Congo basin, are therefore a major issue for the future of humanity as a whole.

They are consequently a shared asset for which we are jointly responsible. The conservation of the Congo basin, the world's second ecological lung after the Amazon basin, is clearly a requirement for our collective survival.

– V –

Opening speech at the
6th World Sustainable Development Forum
(Brazzaville, 29th October 2008)
(Extracts)

(...) The protection of nature is a costly business, but no price can be put on it. It brings dividends that will benefit future generations.

To our African sisters and brothers who have done me the honour and favour of coming here, I would like to make a concrete proposal. I suggest that we create an African Fund for Sustainable Development, to which each of our countries will be called on to contribute according to their means and in accordance with rules to be determined. The sums we deposit will form a guarantee of our commitment and attract outside contributions.

(...) An excellent example of North-South dialogue, with participants examining an issue of vital global interest, the Brazzaville Forum offers a perfect illustration of the interdependence between human societies.

For two days, experts and personalities from all over the African continent, Europe, America and Asia have made diagnoses and suggested solutions. I am particular impressed by the powerful content of their presentations and the quality of their discussions. The comprehensive reports that will be presented to Heads of State will provide the latter with a valuable perspective to assist their decision-making. Many of the points emphasised confirm different certainties and convictions. Some refer to issues that still do not receive sufficient consideration, but all go to form a tool for decision-makers, enabling us to make the necessary informed, relevant decisions and set appropriate measures in motion.

The proceedings that have just taken place over two days and the summit that will now begin are valuable in that they keep the flame of hope alive in the heart of an Africa which, despite the gathering clouds, firmly refuses to become the tomb of humanity, having once served as its cradle. An Africa which, in terms of sustainable development, is not the problem, but a part – a large part – of the solution.

Not despair, resignation or inevitability, but lucidity, conviction and solidarity are the watchwords I suggest.

Let us organise ourselves and act !

Let us act quickly and more efficiently as part of the world front confronting environmental challenges and the scourge of poverty.

Let us act quickly to achieve the Millennium Objectives for Development.

Let us act quickly, to forge ahead towards the post-Kyoto horizon and effectively implement the Johannesburg plan of action.

Printed in the USA
September 2009
ISBN: 978-159221-740-3